KwicKode® — Springboard to Python

Learn to Program in Just Three Days

by
Dan Bishop, Ph.D.

Miritish Publishing

KwicKode® —
Springboard to Python

Learn to Program in Just Three Days

Published by Miritish Publishing.

Other Books by Dan Bishop

The Saturn Accords Series:
Saturn Conundrum
Saturn Rendezvous
Saturn Alliance

Mastering Spanish Irregular Verbs

C For Programmers

C-Tools:1

Organic & Biological Chemistry Lab Manual
Laboratory Manual for Organic Chemistry

Credits

Cover Art: Dan Bishop & Microsoft Copilot AI
Cover Fonts: Microsoft Sans Serif and Sans Serif Italics
This book was written and formatted using Microsoft Word
on Windows 11.
Interior fonts by Microsoft:
Times New Roman, Arial, and Courier New

Table of Contents

Introduction to KwicKode®

L earn to code in just three days? Is that even possible? A typical programming course takes a full semester. The twenty-four-hour claim in this book's subtitle sounds nuts, as unbelievable as those get-rich-quick schemes that keep popping up in our emails.

But wait! KwicKode has only sixteen commands, and all are based on common English sentences. That's it. Sixteen English language commands, yet KwicKode is a fully functional computer language. Check out the following sample KwicKode program and try to predict what it does.

```
Comment: Demo0.0 Five KwicKode commands.
Assign "Hello. Welcome to KwicKode." to greeting.
Display greeting.
Assign greeting to list welcome.
Create file starter.csv.
Comment: Your greeting is being saved to disk.
Copy data from welcome to starter.csv.
Comment: Retrieving it now into a new list.
Copy data from starter.csv to saved_msg.
Display saved_msg as list.
```

If you predicted that running Demo0.0 would produce:

```
Hello. Welcome to KwicKode.
Hello. Welcome to KwicKode.
```

you have already learned five of KwicKode's sixteen commands, and in less than five minutes!

KwicKode is an English language overlay for Python, the world's most widely used computer language in 2024. KwicKode's commands follow English language sentence structure, with verbs and objects instead of symbolic notation. The ten-line demo0.0 program above required 38-lines of Python code, most of which would be incomprehensible to someone with no coding knowledge.

Here are four unique advantages you will gain from your three-day dive into KwicKode:

1. KwicKode is the perfect introductory language for students with no computer programming background. It is easy to learn and easy to use.

2. KwicKode can handle moderately complex coding tasks. Chapter 8 contains an interactive Tic-Tac-Toe for Two, complete with text-graphic displays. Chapters 12 and 13 offer two KwicKode programs demonstrating both static and dynamic database applications with interactive menu input and .csv file save and retrieve operations.

3. If learning Python is your goal, KwicKode will give you a running start. KwicKode is an ideal springboard for learning Python, or any other language for that matter. Chapter 14 details the correspondence between the two languages to ease the transition.

4. Large language model AI, like ChatGPT, can now handle many coding jobs. However, the human tasking the AI to create a program must be familiar enough with coding to phrase a workable request. KwicKode provides the knowledge and skills to fill this role.

Eighteen to twenty-four hours of focused study should be sufficient to provide you with a working knowledge of computer programming in general and of KwicKode in particular. With your knowledge of KwicKode, you will have at your disposal a valuable tool that you can use no matter what direction your future may take.

The underlying translator program that makes KwicKode possible is **kk_to_py_translator.py** (© Dan Bishop, 2025) listed in Appendix C and available on request from authordbishop@gmail.com. This program converts your KwicKode programs into Python code that you can then run in a standard Python environment.

kk-to-py-translator.py has its own error checking routine to alert you to common errors. Its messages include the error's line number to help you find the problems easily and quickly make corrections. The program displays all the errors it finds at once, instead of the one-error-per-run approach, a tremendous time-saver. Two examples are:

```
Error in line 5: Statement needs a capital
              letter or an ending period.
Error in line 12: Keyboard input command
              syntax is 'Get string for...'
```

This manual covers KwicKode's sixteen commands with demonstration programs for each. Study and run each program, then create several of your own using the demo programs as guides. Move on only when you feel you fully understand how they work and what they are used for. Appendix A lists all sixteen commands, showing the syntax for each. You may wish to tab the page for quick reference.

Before You Begin

This section details how to install the latest stable Python package into your computer and then load and test the **kk_to_py_translator.py** program that converts KwicKode programs into Python code. Follow the steps below and you'll be ready to roll before you know it.

A. Download the Python package from https://www.python.org. Select your operating system and choose the most recent stable installer program for your computer (e.g. Windows installer 32 bit) and download it. In your Downloads folder, double click on the executable installer, such as 'python-3.12.8-amd64.exe' and install your package. Select 'Yes' to place icons on your desktop or task bar so they are easy to find.

B. The Python package includes the IDLE shell program and the IDLE editor. Click on the Python icon you just installed, and the IDLE shell window appears. This window is where all program output, both from KwicKode and from Python, will be displayed, as well as prompts for keyboard entry and cursor control.

C. Select File→New File. A new empty window appears, labelled 'Untitled'. This is the IDLE editor window where you type in your program text, like using a word processor.

D. Next, install the **kk_to_py_translator.py** program. This is the program that translates your KwicKode programs into Python code so you can run them. If you are using the online version of this manual, highlight the entire program in Appendix C, press <Ctrl-C> to copy it, then click the

cursor in the empty IDLE editor window and press
<Ctrl-V> to paste the program into the editor.

E. Click File➔Save As to save the translator program. This is
the only time you will have to type in the full name. But be
sure to include the '.py' suffix! This tells the Python
interpreter that it is a Python program file.

F. Select RUN➔Run Module in the editor window to run the
program. If it copied correctly, you will see the prompt:

```
Enter the name of your KwicKode text file...
```

Just press <Enter> (ignore any error messages) and close
the editor window. Your copy is ready to go.

G. If you did not get the prompt shown in Step F, your
translator program copy needs a bit of editing. The
problems are probably due to ragged indents. Check the
highlighted line and compare it to the listing in Appendix
C for guidance. Add or delete spaces to adjust the line for
the proper indent, and correct any others you see. Then try
Run➔Run Module again and repeat the process. It may
take several tries before the Python interpreter is happy.

Your coding environment is now set up for your
KwicKode experience. You've done well! If it's Friday night
and you've set aside a three-day weekend for this exciting
adventure, get a good night's sleep. and be ready to jump into
KwicKode tomorrow morning. Your whole life is about to
change!

Chapter 1
Output and Comments

```
Comment: Hello World intro program.
Display "Hello World!".
```

KwicKode commands use simple English language sentences. Commands that don't initiate or end a block of code (Chapter 4) always begin with a capital letter and end with a period. They include a verb and an object. KwicKode programs read like a storybook.

Computer Output

The two-line program above demonstrates a 'Comment:' statement and the KwicKode output command, 'Display', which sends the command's object (in this case, the text 'Hello World!') to IDLE's shell window to be displayed. Computer **output** refers to any information flow from the computer to the outside world. Besides the monitor, this includes printers, mechanical devices, communication controls, maybe even your refrigerator!

The format rules, or **syntax**, required for the 'Display' command is the word 'Display' followed by one or more items, called **objects**, separated by commas, and ending in a period. Text objects must be surrounded by quotation marks and are called **strings**. Objects may also be numbers, expressions (like 2+2 or 12/3) which may be enclosed in parentheses for visual clarity, and variables (Chapter 2). Note that the word 'and' is NOT included if there are multiple objects. The last character in the sentence must be a period.

```
Comment: Demo1.1-Multiple Output Objects.
Display "At",1000, "dollars a ticket, ".
Display "a full stadium of",70000, "fans".
Display "would gross",70, "million dollars! ".
```

Notice the periods at the end of every line, even though they may look odd when they are preceded by text punctuation. If you try to run a program with missing periods, the translator program will kindly send you an error message.

```
Comment: Demo1.2-Lame joke output.
Display "Why did the scarecrow receive an award?".
Display "Because he was out standing in his field.".
```

If you want quotes within a string, use single quotes. If you want a line-break, either use two 'Display…' commands, or place a backslash-n: '\n' within the string. Multiple blank lines can be achieved with multiple \n's in a 'Display…' string, or by displaying an empty string:

```
Comment: Demo1.3-Line breaks.
Display "A 2 line\n\n break, or use".
Display "".
Display "Display with an empty string. ".
```

Comments and Documentation

KwicKode requires the first line of every program to be a 'Comment:' statement. Thus, every program is graced with a title or description and may include author and date.

'Comment:' statements may appear anywhere within your program. They are totally ignored by the computer, so quotes aren't necessary (but the colon and period are.) You should use as many comments as you need to describe code constructs or to provide descriptive subtitles for different sections of a program. If two or more comment lines are needed to cover a long comment statement, every line must begin with the word 'Comment:' and end with a period.

Giving your program a title in the first line establishes an early focus on documentation. Documenting your programs is an essential part of programming. Consider a 1000-line program you might write sometime in the future. Six months later, you may want to modify the program. Without documentation, you could spend many hours trying to figure out what you did six months earlier. Proper documentation, however, will direct you right to the parts that need editing, and the coding will proceed with far fewer glitches. Good documentation is a real lifesaver for anyone else having to edit your program as well.

Compiling and Running Your Programs

So, now you have the code for two-KwicKode programs. Time to run them and see first-hand what they do!

First, enter the code for one of the programs into an empty IDLE editor window by typing it in or using copy-and-paste, then save it as a text file. (That is, follow the name with a '.txt' suffix, as in 'hello.txt'.) Next load and run the **kk_to_py_translator.py** program you saved earlier. Use File→Recent Files and click on the program's name to load it. A new IDLE window opens and fills with the translator program code. Run the translator by clicking that window's Run→Run Module menu option. The translator program will ask you to enter the name of the text file to be translated (no need to type the .txt suffix here, so 'hello' will do). If there are no errors, you will see the message:

```
Your Python program named  hello.py
is ready to run.
```

(Note the .py suffix. This is a genuine Python program.)

After you have translated your KwicKode file and are told that the Python version is ready to run, click File→Open in the SHELL window, type in the name of your program with the '.py' suffix instead of '.txt'. A new window appears with the Python version of your program. Since you aren't yet studying Python, don't pay any attention to the Python code (unless you are just curious.) But click on Run→Run Module in the Python program's window to run the program. Your output will appear in the SHELL Window. If an error message appears now, the message will refer to the Python program, and will probably be unintelligible. If you encounter an error here, go back to your KwicKode program and review it very carefully to try to find what went wrong and make corrections.

However, if all goes well (no errors in the Python code), the phrase 'Hello World!' appears as output in the shell window. You have entered, **compiled**, and run your first KwicKode program!

Follow these same steps for the second three-line program, using a name of your own choosing (such as 'dumb_joke.txt'.)

General computer note: The only 'language' your computer understands is **machine code**, an incomprehensible series of ones and zeros, such as '0010100101001101'. So-called **higher-level languages** that humans can understand must ultimately be converted into machine code, usually through several steps. This is done by one of two processes. A **compiler** is a translator program that translates your program (in KwicKode) into a program one-step lower (Python). Then you must load and run the Python program. The other method starts with a higher-level program and translates it line-by-line in real time all the way down to machine language and executes each line right away with no intermediate program to load and run. The program that does this is called an **interpreter**. Your Python package has an interpreter that runs Python programs in real time.

Below are some additional jokes for you to enter, compile and run. Or, you may have other text ideas you would like to enter. Each program must initially be entered into a blank editor window created by selecting the File→New File menu option. Write and run several of these programs until you are comfortable with the procedure.

Why don't skeletons fight each other?
They don't have the guts.

Why did the bicycle fall over?
It was two-tired!

What do you call fake spaghetti?
An impasta!

What did one wall say to the other?
'I'll meet you at the corner!'

These steps for compiling and running your KwicKode programs are listed in the box on the next page in full detail, outlining the procedure you will be using throughout the course for developing and executing KwicKode programs. The page after shows this procedure in a visual diagram. You may want to tab this page for quick reference, although you'll soon be doing this with your eyes closed.

Writing and Executing KwicKode Programs

1. **Write and edit your KwicKode program** in the Python IDLE editor window as if you were using a word processor. Save it with a unique name that includes the .txt suffix. To execute saves later on, press <Ctrl-S>.

2. **Load and run the kk_to_py_translator.py program** using File→Open or File→Recent Files to load it, then select Run→Run Module to run it.

3. **Enter the name of your program** when prompted. You may omit the .txt suffix.

4. If your program has errors, the translator lists them for you and gives you their line numbers, making it easy for you to make edits. Return to step 1, **correct the errors in your KwicKode program, and try again.**

5. **If there are no errors**, the translator tells you your program is ready to run. **Load the Python version of your program** using File→Open or File→Recent Files and enter or select your program with the .py suffix attached. For example, hello.py.

6. **Run the Python version of your program**: Select Run→Run Module. All output, including requests for input (Chapter 3) will appear in the shell window. If Python detects errors, **close the window containing the .py version of your program (important!)** Then, if necessary, reload your KwicKode .txt program and return to step 1 to find and correct the errors.

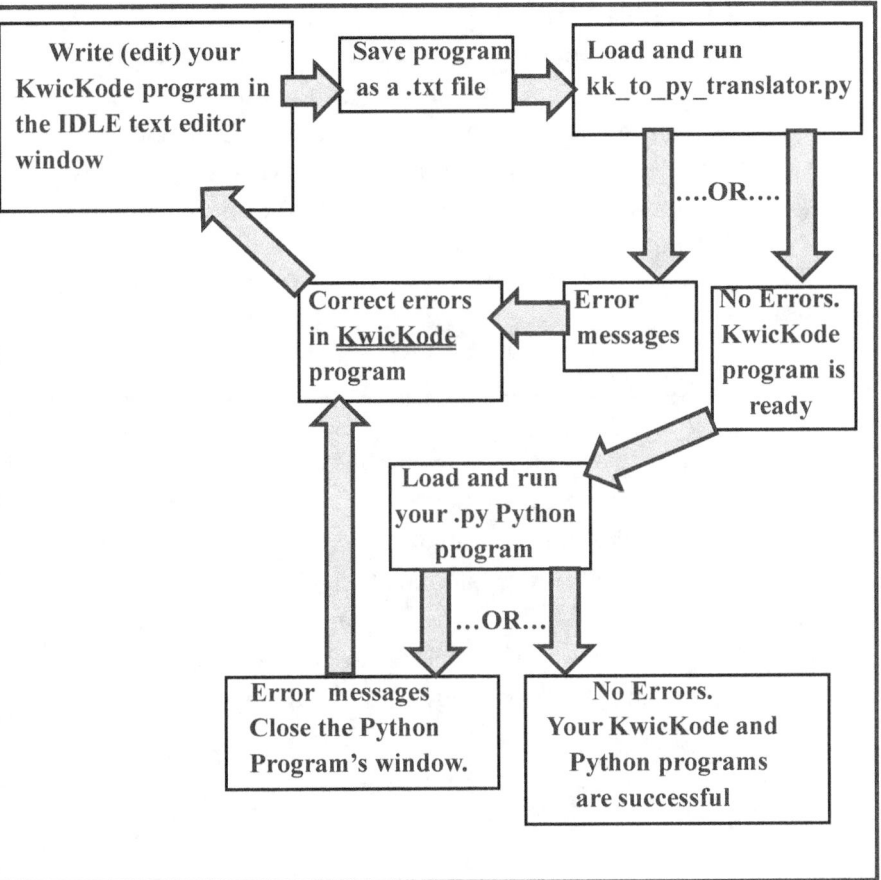

Schematic Diagram for Running a KwicKode Program

There is one variation for the 'Display…' command that you will encounter later (Chapter 7) that deals with lists and list output. That version adds the words 'as list' to the end of the command, as in:

```
Display members_names as list.
```

Using this variation creates a vertical listing of the elements within the list. But here's a fun thing you can do with it now. Using the line above (with a 'Comment:', of course) replace 'members_names' with a short string and see what happens when you compile and run the program! This exercise shows that KwicKode (and Python) consider strings to be lists of single characters!

In this lesson you have learned how to enter, save, and translate a KwicKode computer program, converting it into a Python program. You now know how to load and run the Python programs the translator creates.

You have also learned how to use two KwicKode commands, and the meaning of the following computer terms:

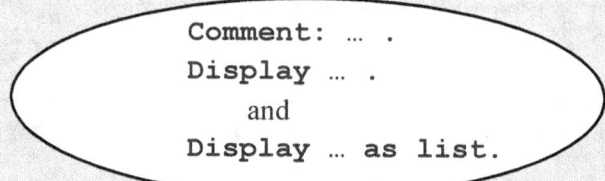

```
Comment: … .
Display … .
      and
Display … as list.
```

output	string	object	syntax
compiler	interpreter	documentation	
machine code		higher-level language	

Chapter 2
Variables and Assignments

```
Comment: Demo2.1 Assignment statements & variables.
Assign "Gonzo" to my_pet.
Assign "gorilla" to pet_type.
Assign 12 to pets_age.
Display "My pet, ",my_pet, ", is a",pet_type, ".".
Display my_pet, "is",pets_age, "years old. ".
Comment: Note that every line ends in a period.
```

Variables and assignments go hand-in-hand. Variables are objects that contain information, and assignments are the commands that place information into the variables. It thus makes sense that the two subjects be covered in the same chapter.

Variables

Think of a variable as a label you put on a drawer that contains one or more pieces of data. You want the label to reflect what is stored in the drawer, but the actual item(s) in the drawer can be changed whenever necessary.

So, in the program above, the variables my_pet, pet_type, and pets_age are labels for memory locations that hold your pet's name, its species, and its age. In your programs, you can create whatever names you want for your many variables so long as you abide by the following rules.

The Variable Rules:

Rules for naming variables in KwicKode are the same as those for Python. Only lower-case letters, numbers, and the underscore are allowed but the variable must begin with a letter. Spaces are not allowed, so multiple words must be connected with an underscore, such as 'pets_age'. Variable names cannot be words that are reserved words in either KwicKode (such as 'display', 'comment', and 'assign') or in Python (such as 'print' and 'input'.) If you accidentally use a reserved word, you will receive an error message in the shell window.

(If rules are variable, can they really be rules?)

In general, it is helpful to come up with variable names that indicate what values they will be representing, such as my_pets or new_member. With KwicKode's command lines reading like English sentences, inventing appropriate names to fit into the sentences is a natural process.

The Assignment Command

Demo2.1 illustrates KwicKode's 'Assign ... to ...' command used for assigning values to variables. The first ellipsis represents the value, either a string, a number, an expression or a variable name. The second ellipsis is for the variable name you create to represent that value.

Practice writing several KwicKode programs that display favorite poems, song lyrics, nursery rhymes, etc., using 'Display' and 'Assign' commands and comments. With special characters (in quotes) such as '+++||+++', you can create simple stick-figures and images, even a Christmas tree! These are known as **'text graphics'**.

```
Comment: Demo2.2-Text Graphics.
Display "     +          *".
Assign "/ \\" to peak.
Assign "/    \\" to roof.
Assign "|    |" to house.
Display "    ",peak, "     ***".
Display "    ",roof, "    *****".
Display "    ",house, "     |".
```

(Note: Some special characters, like the backslash, must be preceded by a backslash to display properly.)

Two interesting features for strings is that they can be multiplied, and they can be glued to each other with the '+' operator, a process known as **concatenation**. So, (a + b) becomes 'I feel great!' if 'I feel' has been assigned to a, and ' great!' has been assigned to b. Later, if you are under the weather, just assign ' awful.' to b and run the program again.

```
Comment: Demo2.3 Multiplying strings.
Assign "*" to stars.
Assign "=" to equals.
Assign (equals + stars + equals) to combo.
Display stars*12.
Display equals*12.
Display combo*4.
```

For pictures, write your code such that repeated sequences are assigned to variables (as in the above example) and your 'Display' lines use the variables to help draw the image.

```
Comment: Demo2.4-String Concatenation.
Display "Demo 2.4    String Concatenation".
Assign "Michelangelo" to artist.
Assign "Sistine Chapel" to church.
Assign (str(1510)) to date.  ⟵▅▅▅▅
Assign (artist+" painted the "+church) to msg1.
Assign (" ceiling in " + date + ".") to msg2.
Display msg1 + msg2.
```

Note the use of the str(...) **function** (borrowed from Python) in the date assignment statement. This is a 'type-conversion' function that turns numbers into strings. This was necessary so that the '1510' could be concatenated along with the other strings. Concatenation only works with strings. Two other type conversions functions you will find useful are the int(...) function that converts strings to integers if the string does not include a decimal point (an error results otherwise) and the float(...) function that converts the string to a decimal number.

```
Comment: Demo2.5-Concatenation & str(...) function.
Assign 21 to my_age.
Assign 26 to sisters_age.
Display "My sister is ", sisters_age.
Display "and I am ", my_age, ".".
Assign (sisters_age - my_age) to age_diff.
Assign ("My sister is "+str(age_diff)) to msg.
Display (msg + " years older than me. ").
```

Math Operations

Expressions in KwicKode follow the simple rules of arithmetic and algebra. The common math operators '+', '-', and '/' are accompanied by '*' for multiplication and '**' for exponentiation, where '**2' squares a number and '**0.5' returns its square root.

In addition, KwicKode will automatically import Python's advanced math module providing trig, log, statistics, and conversion functions if you precede the function name with 'math.' (include the 'dot'). (Math nerds note: Angles must be expressed in radians.) For example:

```
Assign leg1 * math.tan(angle) to leg2.
```

> **General Computer Note**: The IDLE shell window does a lot more than display output. It serves as a window to the entire world of Python. Where it serves KwicKode is in supplying details relating to imported modules. To demonstrate this, enter the command 'import math' after the '>>>' IDLE prompt. Then enter 'help(math)'. An alert appears: 'Squeezed text 309 lines.' Click on the message to open the text and scroll through the long list of math functions you can use in KwicKode and in Python.

```
Comment: Demo2.6 Expressions.
Assign 25 to diameter.
Assign (3.14159 * diameter) to circumference.
Display "The circumference of a ",diameter, " cm".
Display "diameter circle is: ", circumference, "cm.".
```

A frequent coding task is increasing a numeric value by a given amount. Loop counters are a common example. The demo below shows how this is done.

```
Comment: Demo2.7 Counter Implementation.
Assign 39 to my_age.
Display "I am ", my_age, " this year. ".
Comment: Increment the age variable by one.
Assign (my_age + 1) to my_age.
Display "Next year I will be " + str(my_age) + ".".
```

Note that my_age in the first 'Display' line is a separate item and is an integer, while in the second 'Display' line, it is converted to a string so it can be concatenated with the other strings. It is up to you to decide which method to use.

Another useful technique to know is how to round decimal numbers to a desired number of decimal places. The process looks like this:

To reduce 3.14159 to two decimal places:
1. Multiply by 100 and add 0.5 → 314.659.
2. Apply the integer function → 314.
3. Divide by 100 → 3.14.

```
Comment: Demo2.8-Rounding decimal numbers.
Assign (100 / 3) to many_digits.
Display "100/3 equals ",many_digits.
Assign (many_digits * 100 + 0.5) to midway.
Assign (int(midway)) to midway.
Assign (midway / 100) to fewer_digits.
Display many_digits,"is rounded to ",fewer_digits.
```

Careful use of parentheses can combine the three assignment statements into a single line, as in the following.

```
Assign (int(many_digits*100+0.5)/100) to fewer_digits.
```

Before moving on, write at least two programs that use the main concepts that have been covered thus far. Think of various expressions that you can use to fit into your programs. For example: 'How large a bowl will I need for a recipe that calls for 6 cups of flour, 3 cups of milk, a quarter cup of sugar and 3 eggs (another quarter cup) if I want to leave the bowl half empty for stirring?'

Or, 'How far can I drive before running out of gas if my car gets 18 mpg city and 24 mpg country and my trip includes 3 cities for a total of 15 miles? My tank holds 18 gallons.'

In this lesson you have learned about variables and how to assign values to them. You have learned how to use the str(…), int(…), and float(…) functions, how to concatenate strings, and how to round numbers.

You have also learned the following computer terms:

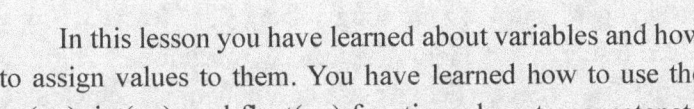

```
Assign … to … .
```

assignment   variable   concatenation
functions   text graphics

Chapter 3
Prompts and Input

```
Comment: Demo3.1 Input Command.
Display "Please enter your name…".
Get string for user_name.
Display "Please enter your age…".
Get string for user_age.
Display "Glad to meet you, ", user_name, ".".
Display "You don't look ", user_age, "!".
Display "In 5 years".
Display "you will be ",(int(user_age)+5),".".
```

The term **input** in computer technology refers to the flow of information from the outside world into the computer for processing. As the name implies, it is the opposite of output. The source of input can be as varied as keyboard entry, an amazing variety of physical sensors, video cameras and audio devices, and much more. Think of all the data-feeds needed to make an autonomous vehicle safe for operation on the highway or to land an airliner without pilot input.

Keyboard entry input operations in KwicKode require two lines. The first is a 'Display…' command like those you've been working with already to display a **prompt** telling the user what type of information is expected. The second is a 'Get string for…' command that captures the information the user has typed in when they press <Enter>. The word 'string' emphasizes that data entered at the keyboard is always of string type (as it is in Python.) After 'for' comes a variable name that will store the value entered. The demo program above illustrates how input works with KwicKode.

Note the use of the int(...) type conversion function in the last line of Demo 3.1 to convert the string 'user_age' to a number so it can be used in a numeric calculation. If a decimal number were desired, the type conversion function would need to be float(...), short for 'floating point', or decimal, number. This issue must be kept in mind whenever a numeric value is called for from the keyboard. Using the int(...) function on a string with a decimal point will cause an error, so if in doubt, use the float(...) function first.

The following example requires three prompts to accompany the three 'Get string for...' input commands. Note that cost, entered as a string, must be converted to a number before it can be used in a math calculation.

```
Comment: Demo3.2 Prompts and input commands.
Display "What are you saving your money for? ".
Get string for object.
Display " How much does this "+object+" cost in $$? ".
Get string for cost.
Comment: Convert cost to a decimal number.
Assign (float(cost)) to cost.
Display "How much can you save each week? ".
Get string for savings.
Assign (float(savings)) to savings.
Assign (cost/savings) to weeks.
Comment: Round weeks to a whole number.
Assign (int(weeks + 0.5)) to weeks.
Assign str(weeks) to weeks.
Display "It will take you "+weeks+" weeks to save ".
Display "enough to buy your ", object, ".".
```

The required 'Display…' command providing the prompt must evaluate to a single string. If you want to use several objects in your prompt, use concatenation and the str(…) function to make the prompt into a single string.

One common use of the keyboard input command is to pause the program. If the variable is a 'dummy' variable, the program will still pause for user input. The prompt for this may simply be: Display "Press <Enter> to continue…".

```
Comment: Demo3.3-Knock-Knock Joke.
Display "Press <Enter> after each pause…".
Display "KNOCK KNOCK".
Get string for blank.
Display "Who's there? ".
Get string for blank.
Display "Armageddon. ".
Get string for blank.
Display "Armageddon who? ".
Get string for blank.
Display "Armageddon tired of Knock-Knock jokes. ".
```

Another common situation occurs when the user's input must be compared to some other string to verify that the input is valid or acceptable, or to use it in a search in a database. Since the user may type in any combination of upper and lower case characters, the usual approach is to have the program convert the input string to all upper or all lower case characters, or, if it is a name, to capitalize just the first characters. This is handled with three methods, '.upper( )', '.lower( )', and '.title( )',respectively. (Note the periods, or 'dots' at the start of each method. Also note that these three methods always have an empty set of parentheses.)

Unlike functions, such as 'str(...)', which place the object to be operated on inside the function's parentheses, **methods** are attached to the object with the 'dot'. So to convert the string 'GonZo', in the variable my_pet to all upper case, all lower case, or just first-character upper case, one of the following case conversion lines would be used.

```
Assign my_pet.upper() to my_pet.
Assign my_pet.lower() to my_pet.
Assign my_pet.title() to my_pet.
```

```
Comment: Demo3.4-Case conversion methods.
Display "Enter one or more words with mixed".
Display "upper and lower case characters. ".
Get string for entry.
Display entry.upper().
Display entry.lower().
Display entry.title().
```

Now, a search through a database for 'Gonzo' after using the '.title( )' method might find a match, whereas searching for 'GonZo' would be futile. (Unless, of course, your pet's name did indeed have a capital 'Z'.)

Rewrite the sister's age program in the previous chapter so that both ages are entered at the keyboard. Each time you run the program, you can input different numbers for different results. Some combination of numbers will produce erroneous output. 'Garbage in, garbage out!' We'll look at one method for dealing with input error problems in the next chapter.

Next, write two or three programs that combine everything you have learned so far. Programs might include calculating the perimeter of a rectangle and its area (where width and length are entered at the keyboard), the miles-per-gallon gas consumption of your vehicle after you have entered the gallons used and the miles driven, or the price of a shirt after a given discount when you have entered the initial price and the discount.

In this lesson you have learned how to incorporate data entered at the keyboard into your program. You can now handle input and output, and you know how to name and work with variables and assign values to them. You can also convert user string input into numbers for use in calculations, and control upper/lower case representation for comparisons.

You have also learned the meaning of the following computer terms:

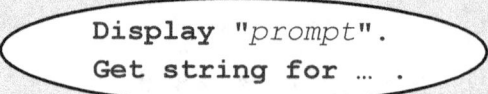

```
Display "prompt".
Get string for ... .
```

input	prompts	methods
.upper( )	.lower( )	.title( )

Chapter 4
Blocks; Conditional Commands

Conditional statements, repeating commands, and functions all involve several lines of code. These multiple command units are called **blocks**, and all of KwicKode's blocks have similar syntax requirements. The most obvious is that the entire block of code is enclosed in square brackets. But there are other similarities as well, such that we might call these the 'Block Theme.'

The Block Theme:

1. The first line begins with a left bracket '[' and ends with a colon instead of a period.
2. The last line is always an 'End of … block.]' statement. The last character in this line is a right bracket ']' to close the block. The ellipsis represents a word that identifies the block being closed, and will be one of these: 'if', 'else', 'function', or 'repeat'.
3. All lines in a block *except the first line* should be indented.

Indenting isn't required in KwicKode, but it is strongly recommended since it is a required feature in Python. It also helps in identifying blocks visually within a large program and is particularly useful when two or more blocks are nested within each other. Note that the 'End of…block.]' statements clearly identify which block is being ended. They will have the same indent as the other lines within that block.

Here is an example of two blocks associated with KwicKode's conditional statements, the subject of this chapter.

```
Comment: Demo4.1 Conditional Statements.
Display "Enter the 4-digit year you were born in...".
Get string for birth_year.
[If (birth_year  < "2000") then:
    Display "Wow! You witnessed a century change.".
    End of if block.]
[Else:
    Display "Sorry you missed the 2000 ".
    Display "Centennial Celebrations.".
    End of else block.]
```

Conditional Statements

Conditional statements give the computer a logical expression that evaluates to either 'True' or 'False'. If the expression is 'True', the lines of code in the '[If...then:' block are executed; if not, they are skipped.

The two conditional commands in KwicKode are '[If...then:' and '[Else:' The '[If' is followed by the conditional expression to be evaluated, the word 'then', and a colon. The '[Else:' command is always the only word on its line of code. The rest of the code in its block is executed only when the condition presented in the preceding '[If' command evaluates to 'False.' The '[Else:' command is optional, but it must be preceded by an '[If' command.

For writing conditional expressions, the conditional operators (==, !=, <, >, <=, and >=) make comparisons possible. The double == symbols are the conditional 'equals', as in '[If a == b then:'. KwicKode uses the double '==' symbol to help condition your thinking for Python. Also note that the '!=' stands for 'does not equal'.

Another example that uses conditional statements:

```
Comment: Demo4.2 Conditional statements.
Display "How old are you?".
Get string for my_age.
Comment: Convert string to an integer.
Assign (int(my_age)) to my_age.
[If (my_age < 16) then:
     Assign (16 - my_age) to age_diff.
     Display "You will have to wait ".
     Display age_diff, " years before".
     Display "getting your driver's license.".
     End of if block.]
[Else:
     Assign (my_age-16) to age_diff.
     Display "So, you have been driving for ".
     Display str(age_diff) + " years!".
     End of else block.]
```

Note that all statements in the two blocks except the first lines are indented for visual clarity.

You can combine several conditional expressions with 'and', 'or', and 'not', as in:

```
[If (my_age > 21 and my_age < 29) then:
```

but each part of the expression must be a complete conditional expression on its own. For example:

```
[If (my_age > 21 and < 29) then:    ERROR!!
```

will produce an error. Both conditions require the variable 'my_age' to be expressed.

Another conditional operator is 'in' and its negative, 'not in' which searches through a string of characters (or a list of objects) to see if a match with a specified character (or object) can be found. This works well for programs that offer the user a menu of choices, as in Demo 4.3.

```
Comment: Demo4.3-Conditional blocks for menus.
Display "Roadkill Pizza Cellar Menu".
Display "A. Spicy Squirrel  B. Rabid Rabbit".
Display "C. BBQ Armadillo   Q. Quit".
Display "Please enter your selection... ".
Get string for choice.
Assign choice.upper() to choice.
[If choice not in "ABCQ" then:
    Display "Invalid choice. Try again. ".
    End of if block.]
[Else:
    [If choice == "A" then:
        Display "With or without olives? ".
        End of if block.]
    [If choice == "B" then:
        Display "Added mushrooms? ".
        End of if block.]
    [If choice == "C" then:
        Display "Extra cheese? ".
        End of if block.]
    End of else block.]
```

Note the conversion of choice to upper case using the '.upper( )' method so the comparisons that follow will work.

Write several short programs similar to those in the examples that use both 'if' and 'else' conditional commands. All of your programs should use keyboard input for values that are then used in the conditional expressions. For at least two of them, include a second 'if/else' set of blocks nested within the first, as in Demo 4.3. You will need two levels of indentation to accomplish this task.

Finally, set up a menu routine of your own with appropriate output for at least four menu options in the prompt. Each time you run the program, select a different option, resulting in a different output statement. If you decide on a restaurant oriented menu, the output for one run might look like this:

```
Which menu would you like to see?
Enter 1 for Moroccan; 2 for Chinese; 3 for Italian.
3
Our Italian dish for today is vegan lasagna.
```

In this lesson you have learned how to set up conditional commands and write conditional expressions. You have learned how KwicKode handles blocks of code and have seen the advantage of indenting blocks.

```
[If cond_expr then:
        Code for when cond_expr is True.
        End of if block.]
[Else:
        Code for when cond_expr is False.
        End of else block.]
```

You have also learned the meaning of the following computer terms:

blocks   conditional expressions
conditional branching   conditional operators.

Chapter 5
Functions

Functions are such an important part of any programming project that it is important for you to learn how to create and use them as soon as you have some confidence with coding basics. Even though your programs at this stage are relatively simple, developing the skill to organize your projects into well-defined functional units will serve you well throughout your programming career. In fact, it is a skill that can be applied to many life-situations outside of computer science as well.

Function Blocks

Simply put, a function is a group of command lines that performs a single, well-defined task, or **function**. Like conditional commands, they are organized into blocks. Typically, function blocks have only a few lines of code, but they can be as long as necessary to get the job done. For example, the syntax validation function in the kk_to_py_translator.py program which sends error messages when it finds a problem with your code is over seventy lines long.

Function blocks in KwicKode, (as in Python where they are called 'function definitions') must appear at the beginning of the program, before the main program code.

If you include comment lines at the start of your main program such as this:

```
Comment: ************************.
Comment: Main Program begins here.
```

it will help remind you that your functions must come before this point in the program. It will also make it easier to locate where to begin reading your programs.

Functions have names, and the name should give some hint as to what the function does. Function names follow the same rules listed earlier for variable names. For example, a function that requests the user to enter a username and password might be called 'get_username'. Following this might be a function called 'validate_pwd'.

Function Calls

To activate a function, it must be called by its name with a 'Call function…' command. Think of functions and their corresponding 'Call function…' commands as two friends shaking hands. As you will see, they are two separate objects that are inseparably linked.

Here is an example of a KwicKode 'Call function…' command that would be placed in the program where the specified function's task needed to be performed.

```
Call function validate_pwd with (pwd) for is_valid.
```

The reason to call a function is to have it perform a specific task, and the function almost always needs some data to work with to perform that task. This information is passed to the function from the function call by listing the variable(s) containing the data inside the parentheses. In the above example, 'pwd' contains the value being sent to the validate_pwd function. The data in this list are referred to as the function call's **arguments**. Arguments may be variables, strings, or numeric constants.

Similarly, when the function has completed its task, there is usually some value it has produced that must be passed back to the function call. That value is passed to the variable named at the end of the 'Call function...' command. In the example above, the variable 'is_valid' obtains the value returned by the validate_pwd function.

A visual diagram of this process may be helpful.

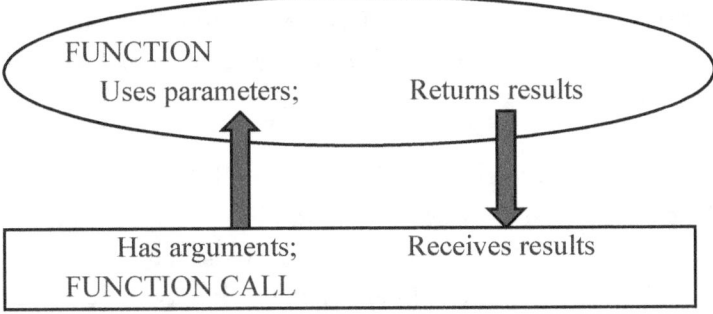

Function Syntax

So, now for the function itself. An example of a function block is shown here.

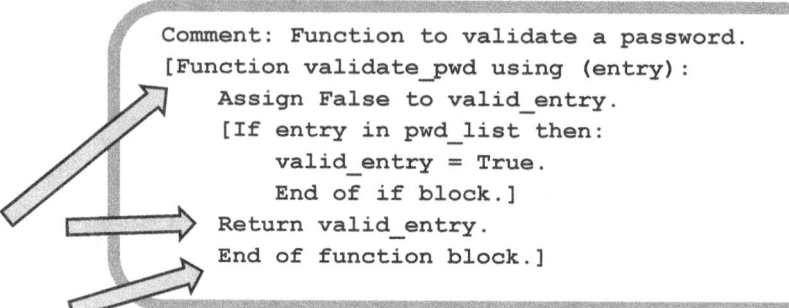

```
Comment: Function to validate a password.
[Function validate_pwd using (entry):
    Assign False to valid_entry.
    [If entry in pwd_list then:
        valid_entry = True.
        End of if block.]
    Return valid_entry.
    End of function block.]
```

KwicKode (like Python) recognizes the words True and False (both capitalized) as reserved word constants with values of 1 and 0 respectively. Thus, they can be used without quotation marks.

Note that the syntax for functions follows the Block Theme described earlier for conditional blocks, with its enclosing set of square brackets, the colon ending the first line, the 'End of function block.]' command as the last line, and the indentation format.

An optional comment line before the function block provides more detail than the sometimes rather cryptic name, and can be very helpful when debugging a program or when going back months or years later to edit the code for tweaks and enhancements.

The first line in a function block has a set of parentheses for a list of variables that are called the function's **parameters.** This list contains the values passed to it from the function call's argument list. Thus, there must be a one-to-one correspondence between the number of arguments in the function call and the number of parameters in the function definition line. In this example, the value in 'pwd' is passed to the variable 'entry' for the function to use.

The variables in the two lists may or may not have the same names. Some Python purists insist that the names must be different to avoid confusing code, but in KwicKode, as in Python, this is totally optional. Both languages isolate what goes on inside a function and once the function has finished executing, all memory relating to its variables is lost. The data and variables within a function are said to be '**local in scope**'. (An important exception to this will be covered in Chapter 7.)

Finally, a function exists to perform a specific task for the 'Call function...' command, and the value resulting from that task must be passed back to the calling command. This is done with the function's 'Return...' command. For the validate_pwd function, 'valid_entry' was determined to be either True or False, and its value is returned to the function call and accepted as 'is_valid'. This is the variable that receives the function's output given by 'Return valid_entry.'

Demo 5.1 puts the above two pieces of code into a full program to help you see how they relate to each other.

```
Comment: Demo5.1-Using functions.

Comment: Function to validate a password.
[Function validate_pwd using (entry,pwd_list):
    Assign False to valid_entry.
    [If entry in pwd_list then:
        Assign True to valid_entry.
        End of if block.]
    Return valid_entry.
    End of function block.]

Comment: ***********************.
Comment: Main Program begins here.
Assign "123PassWord" to pwd_list.
Display "Enter your password.".
Get string for pwd.
Call function validate_pwd with (pwd, pwd_list) for is_valid.
[If is_valid == True then:
    Display "You may enter the Krazy Kingdom.".
    End of if block.]
[Else:
    Display "Your password is bogus. BEGONE!".
    End of else block.]
```

Of course, a real password validation program would have the member passwords encoded in a special database with a different password for each member. We'll see how this can be done in Chapters 12 and 13 after covering lists in Chapter 7. But for this simple demo program, the password is written into the program with an 'Assign' command.

Function calls may appear both in the main program (as above) and in function blocks as well. Thus, functions may call other functions. (They may even call themselves in what is known as a **recursive** process. But if care isn't taken, recursion can lead to a bottomless pit with no return. Incidentally, if your program ever does 'hang', you can press <Ctrl-C> to force it to halt.)

Another function and conditional command example:

```
Comment: Demo5.2 Function calls.

[Function sell using (shares):
    Assign 0.84 to price.
    Assign price*shares to val.
    Return val.
    End of function block.]

[Function hold using (shares, cur_price):
    Assign 2*shares to split1.
    Assign 2*split1 to split2.
    Assign 7*split2 to split3.
    Assign 4*split3 to split4.
    Assign cur_price*split4 to val.
    Return val.
    End of function block.]

Comment: ***********************.
Comment: Main program begins here.
Display "It is Jan. 2, 2000. You have 200 shares of Apple".
Display "Enter today's closing price for Apple. ".
Get string for cur_price.
Assign float(cur_price) to cur_price.
Display "Should you have sold in 2000 or waited? (S/W) ".
Get string for entry.
Assign entry.upper() to entry.
[If entry == "S" then:
    Call function sell with (200) for proceeds.
    End of function block.]
[Else:
    Call function hold with (200, cur_price) for proceeds.
    End of function block.]
Display "Your decision resulted in $",proceeds, ".".
```

Note that if no value is returned by the function, a 'Return' command is still needed, but an empty set of quotes signifies that no value is being passed back to the calling statement. The function call also needs a variable to fulfill syntax requirements. It too will have a blank value, so a 'dummy' variable like 'blank' or 'z' can be used.

The following program is designed to allow you to compare costs for a trip to Seattle by car or by air. The program illustrates the power of functions and how their function calls can be integrated into conditional blocks.

```
Comment: Demo5.3 Trip to Seattle.

[Function by_car using ():
    Display "Enter distance to Seattle in miles: ".
    Get string for dist.
    Assign float(dist) to dist.
    Display "Enter mpg rating for your vehicle: ".
    Get string for mpg.
    Assign float(mpg) to mpg.
    Display "Enter distance you drive per day: ".
    Get string for mpday.
    Assign float(mpday) to mpday.
    Assign int(dist/mpday+.5) to days.
    Assign (days-1)*120 to lodging.
    Assign days*3*15 to meals.
    Assign (dist/mpg)*3.50 to gas.
    Assign (gas+meals+lodging)*2 to cost.
    Display "Assuming $120/day lodging, $3.50".
    Display "gas and $15/day for meals, a round trip".
    Return int(cost).
    End of function block.]
```

```
[Function by_air using ():
    Display "Enter round trip airfare to seattle: ".
    Get string for fare.
    Assign float(fare) to fare.
    Display "Enter daily fee for car rental: ".
    Get string for rpday.
    Assign float(rpday) to rpday.
    Display "Enter days you plan to stay in Seattle: ".
    Get string for days.
    Assign int(days) to days.
    Display "Enter daily fee for airport parking: ".
    Get string for pkpday.
    Assign float(pkpday) to pkpday.
    Assign days*rpday to ttl_lease.
    Assign days* pkpday to ttl_prkg.
    Assign fare+ttl_prkg+ttl_lease to cost.
    Display "Your round trip ".
    Return int(cost).
    End of function block.]


Comment:****************************.
Comment: Main Program Begins Here.
Display "Trip to Seattle Comparison.".
Display "Are you driving (D) or flying (F)? ".
Get string for choice.
Assign choice.upper() to choice.
[If choice == "D" then:
    Call function by_car with () for tripcost.
    Assign "car" to mode.
    End of if block.]
[If choice == "F" then:
    Call function by_air with () for tripcost.
    Assign "air" to mode.
    End of if block.]
[If choice in "DF" then:
    Display "by "+mode+" to Seattle will cost".
    Display "about $",tripcost,"with the info given.".
    End of if block.]
[Else:
    Display "That is not a valid entry. Try again.".
    End of else block.]
```

Rather than repeating the final two lines in the report for each of the two conditional blocks, a third conditional block allows them to appear only once. For this to work, however, a new variable, 'mode', is introduced and given the value 'car' or 'air' just after the function calls.

When reading a program for the first time, find where the main program begins and start reading there. Then you will be able to follow the logic within the program and appreciate how it is organized. When you come to a function call, 'bookmark' that point in the code and go to the function, read through it, and then return to your bookmark. That way you will be taking the same path as the computer, and you will be able to better understand what is going on.

Don't be daunted by a program's length. Computers can only digest one tiny command at a time. So, even relatively simple tasks require a lot of tiny steps. At least with KwicKode, you can read them like a novel.

You have now covered ten of the sixteen KwicKode commands. Program Demo5.3 includes everything you have learned thus far. Study it carefully and review anything in it that you don't fully understand.

Rework each of the exercises using conditional statements that you wrote in Chapter 5, using separate functions for each of the conditional outcomes and placing function calls in the main program where needed for activating the respective function.

In this lesson you have learned how to write functions and function calls and how to organize your program to make effective use of functions.

```
[Function name using (parameters):
      Code to carry out function's task.
      Return result.
      End of function block.]
                and
Call function name with (arguments) for var.
```

You have also learned the meaning of the following computer terms:

function   function call   return values
function blocks   parameters   arguments
scope   recursive

Chapter 6
Loops

Repeating blocks of code are the lifeblood of computer processing. Consider a program that addresses labels for a newsletter publisher's customers. The customer list may have 15,000 records. The program must read a customer's record and print the mailing label. Then it must cycle back to the start and read the next customer record and print another label. The loop must be repeated 15,000 times without human intervention.

There are two common types of loops. The **iterative, or counting loop**, executes the lines of code within the loop's block a specific number of times. A counter is included as part of the loop which can be used as a reference within the loop, for example to enumerate objects in a displayed list or to serve as index values for objects within a list (Chapter 7).

The second loop type is the **conditional loop**, in which the loop's commands are executed so long as a specified condition remains true. If a counter is needed for the conditional loop, most languages require the user to write lines of code to set up and increment the counter.

KwicKode supports both loop types with a single command and maintains a counter variable specified by the programmer for both. Unlike most languages, KwicKode's loop counter is available for use like any other program variable, both inside the loop and beyond, if desired.

The KwicKode Loop Command

The syntax for the KwicKode loop command is:

```
[Repeat block while condition with var:
    Code lines to be repeated.
    End of repeat block.]
```

The first line begins with a left bracket and ends with a colon, as with all blocks in KwicKode. The loop block ends with an 'End of repeat block.]' line, and the code within the block may optionally be indented, making visual identification of the loop instructions obvious.

The conditional expression in the command can be any conditional expression as described in Chapter 4. All the conditional operators, as well as 'and','or', 'not', 'in', and 'not in' may be used. The code within the loop will be executed so long as the conditional expression evaluates to True. When the condition proves false, program controls jumps to the first line after the 'End of repeat block.]' line, ending the loop.

Obviously, something within the loop must change during one of the cycles that will make the conditional expression evaluate to False. Otherwise, the loop will never end! Your program will spin into the 'infinite loop' merry-go-round. Incidentally, if this should happen, the program will appear to 'hang'. Press <Ctrl-C> to halt the program mid-stream.

The *var* is the variable name you choose to be the **counter** for the loop. Avoid 'counter' or 'index', as these are reserved words. But 'cntr' and 'idx' work fine. You must follow the keyword 'with' with a variable name, whether you plan to use a counter or not. A dummy variable such as 'z' can serve this purpose if a counter is not needed.

KwicKode automatically initializes your specified counter variable to zero at the start of the first loop, and automatically increments it by one at the end of each cycle. The reason for starting at zero will become obvious in Chapter 7 when we look at list indexing.

For an iterative loop, the conditional expression may use your counter variable and compare it to a number one larger than the number of times you want the loop to cycle. (This is because counting starts at zero.) So if you want to set up an iterative loop that cycles 10 times, the following command would be used:

```
[Repeat block while cntr < 10 with cntr:
```

The counter automatically starts at zero and is incremented by one at the end of each cycle. When the counter reads '9', the loop is on its tenth iteration, so the next time the conditional expression is encountered, 'cntr' will be 10 and the expression will evaluate to 'False', ending the loop after ten cycles.

The variable may be used within the cycle as any other variable, and, unlike Python, it can also be changed within the cycle and even used once the loop has terminated. For example, if you wish to increment by two rather than by one, simply add the following line before the 'End of repeat block.]' command:

```
Assign cntr+1 to cntr.
```

If you want to break out of the loop before it cycles fully, reset the counter to a value that will kill the loop:

```
[If friends_name == search_name then:
     Assign cntr + 9999 to cntr.
```

Demo 6.1 for a travel agent illustrates KwicKode's loop command for both conditional and iterative controls. The **menu function** provides five choices from which to choose. Each choice would presumably lead to other functions. But the menu also will simply recycle if the user enters an invalid response, but only five times before it defaults to exiting the function.

```
Comment: Demo6.1 While loops.
[Function menu using (name):
   Assign "0" to entry.
   Assign "123456" to opts.
   [Repeat block while entry not in opts with cntr:
      Display "Name your destination, ",name,". ".
      Display "1. Ireland  2. Turkey  3. Japan".
      Display "4. Mexico   5. Norway  6. Quit".
      Get string for entry.
      [If cntr > 4 then:
         Assign "6" to entry.
         End of if block.]
      End of repeat block.]
   Return entry.
   End of function block.]
```

```
Comment: Main Program.
Display "Please enter your first name. ".
Get string for name.
Call function menu with (name) for ans.
[If (ans in ("12345")) then:
   Display "Good choice. More info to follow. ".
   End of if block.]
[Else:
   Display "Sorry we couldn't help you, ",name,". ".
   Display "Do come again. ".
   End of else block.]
```

'While' loops are useful when the number of loop cycles is varied, as when a particular input is expected. For example, how often have you mistyped a password? The program gives you an error message, then loops back to the input process. When you have provided the correct password, the loop ends and the program resumes from there.

Demo 6.2 is a game that reflects how the conditional loop can be implemented. The program chooses a random number from 0 to 9 and asks you to try to guess the number chosen. The loop continues until you guess right or give up in disgust and enter 'Q' to quit. (If you press the same number successively, it might take 20 or 25 tries before the random generator comes up with your number.

```
Comment: Demo6.2. Guess the number.
Assign "0123456789" to options.
Assign "" to ans.
Assign "11" to guess.
[Repeat block while ans != guess and cntr<100 with cntr:
   Assign choice(options) to ans.
   Display "Guess the number I'm thinking of. ".
   Display "Enter 0 to 9, or 'Q' to quit. ".
```

```
Get string for guess.
[If guess.upper() == "Q" then:
  Assign 999 to cntr.
  Display "Thanks for playing. Bye. ".
  End of if block.]
[If guess == ans then:
  Display "Fantastic. You got the right number.".
  Display "(Out of ",cntr+1, "tries.)".
  End of if block.]
End of repeat block.]
```

The random selection function 'choice(...)' can be used with strings or with lists. It is quite useful for games and educational quiz programs. Imagine using 'choice(...)' with a list of 1000 geography questions to generate a random ten-question quiz. More about random functions in Chapter 7.

When combined with lists (next chapter), loops come into their own. The list may be a membership database, a newsletter subscriber list, a list of quiz questions (with answers) for a class, an inventory list, etc. The possibilities are endless.

With a loop, every item in the list can be treated identically (such as raising retail prices by 5% across the board) or an entire list can be searched to locate one specific record for editing or deleting. The remaining chapters are filled with examples of program loops with '[Repeat block while...:' commands, so it's time we jumped right into lists and list operations.

Write a program that uses an iterative loop in which the loop counter is displayed with each cycle through the loop. Then write a program that uses a conditional loop where the loop counter is not included in the conditional expression, but where it is used to determine when to change one of the variables in order to end the loop.

Finally, rework the previous program so that the loop calls a function where the loop counter, passed to it as an argument, is used to determine when to change one of the variables, passing it back in the 'Return' and ending the loop.

In this lesson you have learned how to set up conditional loops and iterative loops. Every loop command line includes a loop counter that you can use both inside the loop block and outside it once the loop has terminated.

```
[Repeat block while (condition) with var:
    Block of code to be repeated.
    End of repeat block.]
```

You have also learned the meaning of the following function and computer terms:

choice(...)   **conditional loops**   **iterative loops**
                   loop counters   **menu functions**

Chapter 7
Lists

L ists are one of the most useful data structures in any computer language. You can do an amazing number of things with lists. Lists also provide a useful format for saving data (Chapters 9, 10, and 12.) Given their importance, they are the one data structure supported by KwicKode and you will encounter them in all the remaining program examples in this manual.

Lists and List Indexing

A **list** is a series of **comma separated objects** presented sequentially that are assigned to a single variable name. The individual elements are accessed by following the variable name with a number enclosed in square brackets, such as my_friends[4], sometimes read as 'my friends sub four', reflecting the mathematical representation 'my_friends$_4$' with a subscript. Because of this similarity, simple lists are often likened to one-dimensional arrays.

The true value of lists lies in taking advantage of the index values associated with the individual elements. You can use index values in a variety of ways, most usually in coordination with a loop command, where the loop counter is used as an index number. For example, the individual objects in a list can be displayed in sequence using an iterative loop.

Index numbering for KwicKode begins at 0, the same as in Python. Thus my_friends[4] is the fifth name in the my_friends list. The square bracket notation is also shared with Python.

There are three ways to create a list in KwicKode. The most obvious way is to use the 'Create list ...' command:

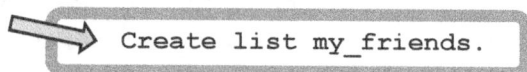

```
Create list my_friends.
```

This command creates an empty list that can then be filled by using the 'Add...to list...' command (see below). The 'Create list' command can also be used to empty an existing list of its contents so it can be filled again with a new set of values.

Two alternatives to 'Create list...' serve to both create a list and add objects to it at the same time. The first of these uses the by-now-familiar assignment statement, with the variable name preceded by the word 'list':

```
Assign a, b, c to list my_list.
```

The objects placed in the list may be of any type, and may even be of mixed types. If the list already exists, its old contents are overwritten.

The second alternative is discussed in relation to file I/O (Chapter 9), where the components of a file are copied to a list. There again, if the list already exists, the copy operation overwrites the old values. If the list doesn't exist, it is created as part of the copy command.

The data in a list may be all of one type (e.g. all strings, such as names) or of mixed types (names and ages), just as in Python. Objects may be strings, numbers, expressions, variables, or even other lists (Chapter 12)! Chapter 10 shows how two or more lists may be linked based on keeping their index numbers synchronized.

```
Comment: Demo7.1-List Operations.
Create list friends.
Add "Bill","Jane","Tom","Sue" to list friends.
Create list moods.
Add "happy","sad","tired","jolly" to list moods.
[Repeat block while k<6 with k:
   Assign choice(friends) to friend.
   Assign choice(moods) to mood.
   Assign "My friend "+friend+" is feeling " to msg1.
   Display msg1+mood+ " today. ".
   Display "Press <enter> to continue.".
   Get string for z.
   End of repeat block.]
```

This program uses the random selection function, 'choice(…)' that randomly chooses one of the objects in the list specified as the function's parameter. (See 'A Random Detour' at the end of this chapter.)

Adding and Removing List Elements

Once you have created a list, you need to add data to it. The 'Add … to list …' command does just that, with the name of your list following the word 'list'. The first ellipsis represents the value(s) to be placed in the list. Several objects may be placed here, separated by commas. (Do not include the word 'and'!) Every new object added is placed at the end of the list.

```
Add "Bill", "Linda", "Jane" to list my_friends.
```

Note the similarity in syntax between this command and the 'Assign...to list...' command. The difference is that this command adds more data to an existing list rather than overwriting the old values.

Normally, a list will be filled (or added to) one element at a time by the user with appropriately prompted 'Get string' commands. The data input is, of course, assigned to a variable that is then used in the corresponding 'Add...to list...' command, as shown below.

```
Assign "" to new_name.
[Repeat block while new_name not in ("Qq") with z:
    Display "Enter a name to add or 'Q' to quit. ".
    Get string for new_name.
    [If new_name not in ("Qq") then:
        Add new_name to list my_friends.
        End of if block.]
    End of repeat block.]
```

Removing items from a list uses the 'Remove...from list...' command. If the item is not found in the list, a message is displayed to that effect. Only one item may be removed at a time.

```
Remove "Bill" from list my_friends.
```

The 'Remove... from list ...' command deletes the first occurrence of the target object. This works well only if all objects in the list are unique. If this isn't the case, you must write a loop to search through the list for a match, display the data for that match, and give the user the option to delete the record displayed or to continue the search.

```
Display "Enter a name to delete from your list. ".
Get string for mean_dude.
Assign "Y" to cont.
[Repeat block while cont == "Y" with cnt:
    [If my_friends[cnt] == mean_dude then:
        Display my_friends[cnt}, emails[cnt], age[cnt].
        Display "Is this the record to be deleted? (Y/N) ".
        Get string for found.
        Assign found.upper() to found.
        [If found == "Y" then:
            Remove mean_dude from list my_friends.
            Display mean_dude, "has been deleted. ".
            End of if block.]
        End of if block.]
    [If cnt >= len(my_friends) and found == "N" then:
        Assign "N" to cont.
        Display mean_dude, "was not found in your list. ".
        End of if block.]
    End of repeat block.]
```

There are two ways in which a list may be displayed. Using the 'Display...' command without the 'as list' add-on will show all the elements in a row, separated by commas, and bracketed on either end with square brackets. On the other hand, using 'Display ... as list.' will present you with a vertical list showing one list element per line.

["Bill", "Linda", "Jane", "Tom", "Sally"]

or, using the 'as list' option:

Bill
Linda
Jane
Tom
Sally

If you want the output to appear differently or to include other related data (from a linked list, perhaps), you will need to create a loop that uses the loop counter as the index number for the displayed elements and format output as desired.

Demo7.2 illustrates working with a list of books (or CDs, etc.) that you might use with your personal collection.

```
Comment: Demo7.2-Add, delete and display lists.
[Function add_book using (my_books):
   Display "Enter a book to add to your list. ".
   Get string for new_book.
   Add new_book to list my_books.
   Return my_books.
   End of function block.]

[Function del_book using (my_books):
   Display "Enter a book to remove from your list.".
   Get string for bad_book.
   Remove bad_book from list my_books.
   Return my_books.
   End of function block.]

[Function show_all using ():
   Display "*"*30.
   Display my_books as list.
   Display "*"*30.
   Return "".
   End of function block.]
```

```
[Function menu using (my_books):
  Assign "N" to quit.
  [Repeat block while quit == "N" with k:
    Display "A to add; D to delete; L to list; ".
    Display "Q to quit. ".
    Get string for choice.
    Assign choice.upper() to choice.
    [If choice == "A" then:
      Call function add_book with (my_books) for my_books.
      End of if block.]
    [If choice == "D" then:
      Call function del_book with (my_books) for my_books.
      End of if block.]
    [If choice == "L" then:
      Call function show_all with () for blank.
      End of if block.]

    [If choice == "Q" then:
      Assign "Y" to quit.
      End of if block.]
    End of repeat block.]
      Return "".
      End of function block.]

  Comment:*************************.
  Comment:Main Program Begins Here.
  Create list my_books.
  Call function menu with (my_books) for blank.
```

Earlier, you learned that variables used inside a function stay inside that function. That is, they had 'local scope'. Lists that are created in the main program (as in 'my_books' above) have a '**global scope**'. What this means is that function calls to functions that use the data in the list but do not change it (as in the 'show_all' function above) do not need to include the list name in their argument list, nor does the function include the name in its parameter list.

List Functions and Methods

KwicKode shares several functions and methods with Python that can be used with lists. These functions may be placed in display or assignment commands or used as part of a conditional expression. One frequently used function you have already encountered with strings is 'len(...)', short for 'length of' in which the list name appears in the parentheses. This function gives the number of objects in a list. For example,

```
Assign len(friends) to friends_count.
```

will assign the number 4 to friends_count if there are four names in the list. Knowing this value gives you a number to use as a cap for looping operations. Keep in mind that the counter starts at 0, so the list-length will always be one higher than the maximum index value available for the list. As a result, index numbers lag a normal counting process by one.

```
[Repeat block while k < len(my_friends) with k:
    Display k+1, ":   ",my_friends[k].
    End of repeat block.]
```

If it's just the index number that you want for an item in your list and every item in the list is unique, you can use the '.index(...)' method borrowed from Python. As mentioned in Chapter 3, methods work much like functions, but their syntax is different. With the 'len(...)' function, the list name appears inside the parentheses. With the '.index(...)' method, (note the period in front of the method name) the list name is attached to the method name with that period, or 'dot', between them and the object in the parentheses is the item whose index number you want.

```
Assign my_friends.index("Tom") to idx.
Display my_friends[idx],":   ",emails[idx].
```

will return Tom's index number and display his name and his email address. This is a great way to search for a specific item in a list, because once you have the index number, you can simply call out the item, as shown above, and if you have a second **linked list** (with synchronized information), the same index number will call out the related data.

If the search object is not unique, you must use a loop to search for Tom, since only the first occurrence of Tom will have its index value returned with the '.index(...)' method. The loop construction you would use would be similar to the example shown above for deleting an item from a list.

One problem with '.index(...)' exists, however, and that occurs when the value being searched for isn't in the list. This situation will cause the program to crash. To keep this from happening, the '.count(...)' method should be used first. Employing this method just before using the '.index(...)' method will return a zero if the item isn't in the list. A simple conditional statement can be used to allow an index search only if the count is not zero.

Add the following function to your Demo-7.2 program, and add an 'S' option to the menu Display line, then add the appropriate conditional block for 'S' containing the function call to this function.

```
[Function search using (my_books):
   Display "Enter a book to search for. ".
   Get string for book.
   Assign my_books.count(book) to cnt.
   [If cnt != 0 then:
      Assign my_books.index(book) to idx.
      Display idx + 1, ": ", my_books[idx].
      End of if block.]
   [Else:
      Display name, "is not in my_friends list. ".
      End of else block.]
   Return "".
   End of function block.]
```

Heading errors off at the pass is an important part of computer coding. Anticipating what could go wrong, especially when dealing with unpredictable user input, requires thoughtful consideration about how your program will be used once it has been delivered.

Search and Retrieval for Lists

If you don't know whether the list contents are unique, you should use a loop to search the list for specific elements. When the data for a match is found, it can then be displayed and the user can choose to continue the search if that set wasn't the data they were looking for.

Demo 7.3 has such a search function. Run this program several times, and search for names on the list. Be sure to search for 'Scout' and answer 'N' when asked if your pet is a dog. The search will then continue until it finds the second instance of 'Scout', the hamster.

```
Comment: Demo7.3 Search in a linked list.

[Function search using (name):
   Display "Searching for ", name.
   Assign -1 to indx.
   [Repeat block while idx < len(my_pets) with idx:
      [If (my_pets[idx] == name) then:
          Display "Is your pet a",pet_type[idx],"?".
          Display "Enter Y or N...".
          Get string for ans.
          [If ans == "Y" or ans == "y" then:
             Assign idx to indx.
             Comment: Set idx to max to end loop.
             Assign len(my_pets) to idx.

             End of if block.]
          End of if block.]
      End of repeat block.]
   Return indx.
   End of function block.]


[Function fill_lists using (my_pets,pet_type):
   Add "Smoky","Scout","Choco","Liz" to list my_pets.
   Add "Spot","Scout","Babe","Benny" to list my_pets.
   Add "cat","dog","hamster","goat" to list pet_type.
   Add "cat","hamster","pig","dog" to list pet_type.
   Return "".
   End of function block.]


Comment:*******************************.
Comment: Main Program Begins Here.
Create list my_pets.
Create list pet_type.
Call function fill_lists with (my_pets,pet_type) for z.
Display "What is the pet's name for this search? ".
Get string for name.
Call function search with (name) for indx.
[If indx == -1 then:
    Display "Sorry, ", name, " is not in your list.".
```

```
    End of if block.]
[Else:
    Display "Your pet ",name, "is pet number ".
    Display (indx+1), "in your list. ", name.
    Display "is a ", pet_type[indx], ".".
    End of else block.]
```

A Random Detour

Demo7.1 randomly selected elements from two unlinked lists to produce totally unpredictable combinations. A random name is picked and a random mood is chosen. As with the 'Guess a Number' game in the previous chapter, this program uses the 'choice(…)' function

This function joins another useful random function, 'shuffle(…)'. The shuffle function randomly re-orders the elements in the list appearing in the parentheses. A dummy variable is used in the assignment command because it is the actual original list that gets randomized. (Be sure to save a copy if you want the original order preserved.)

```
    Assign shuffle(card_deck) to z.
```

The choice function leaves the original list intact. But if you want to make a random selection and remove that object from the list, such as when drawing a card from a deck of cards, the '.pop( )' method comes to the rescue. '.pop( )' takes no parameters. It removes the last item in the attached list for assignment to a variable. So if you create a deck of cards and shuffle it, the '.pop( )' method effectively draws a random card from the deck. The following program demonstrates how this is done.

```
     Assign shuffled_deck.pop( ) to new_card.
```

But be sure to keep track of how many elements you pop from your list. When the list is empty, a '.pop( )' will cause the program to crash.

If you want a random number to be generated between two values, the 'randint(a, b)' function does the trick. In this case, the number generated is returned to the variable specified in the 'Assign...' command line.

```
     Assign randint(0, 100) to rnd_num.
```

Finally, to generate a random decimal number between 0 and 1, the 'random( )' function can be used. This function takes no parameters.

```
     Assign random( ) to rnd_num.
```

```
Comment: Demo7.4-Randomizing Card Selection.
[Function create_deck using (deck):
  Assign "T","J","Q","K","A" to list faces.
  Assign " Hearts"," Spades"," Diamonds"," Clubs" to list suits.
  [Repeat block while suit < 4 with suit:
    [Repeat block while numval < 15 with numval:
      Assign str(numval) to vals.
      [If numval > 9 then:
        Assign faces[numval-10] to vals.
        End of if block.]
      [If numval > 1 then:
        Assign vals + suits[suit] to card.
        Add card to list deck.
        End of if block.]
      End of repeat block.]
    End of repeat block.]
```

```
  [Repeat block while k<13 with k:
    Display deck[k]+" "+deck[k+13]+" "+deck[k+26]+" "+deck[k+39]
    End of repeat block.]
  Display "There are ",len(deck),"cards in this deck.".
  Return deck.
  End of function block.]

[Function draw_card using (deck):
    Assign deck.pop() to card.
    Assign card+" "*30 to msg0.
    Assign msg0[0:15]+" was drawn.   " to msg1.
    Display msg1,len(deck),"cards are left.".
    Return "".
    End of function block.]

Comment: Main Program.
Create list deck.
Call function create_deck with (deck) for deck.
Display "Shuffling cards. Shuffling cards. ".
Display "*"*30.
Assign shuffle(deck)   to z.
[Repeat block while k<52 with k:
   Call function draw_card with (deck) for z.
   End of repeat block.]
```

You can also sort the elements in a list with the '.sort( )' method (no parameters). Like shuffle, the original list gets sorted, so the assignment command uses a dummy variable.

```
Assign my_pets.sort() to z.
```

Write a program that creates a list containing ten objects and uses an iterative loop to display each object along with its index number, such as '8. Flying Saucers'. Code it so that the first object is listed as number one, not zero.

Modify the program so that only even-numbered items are displayed. Finally, modify the program so that the items are displayed in reverse order, counting down from 10 to 1.

Now write a program that creates an empty list and uses the 'Add' and 'Remove' commands in conjunction with user input to add objects to the list and delete objects from the list. A 'Diplay' command should show the resulting list after each operation.

In this lesson you have learned how to create and erase lists, how to add items to lists and delete items from them, and two methods to search through lists for a specific item.

```
Create list listname.
Add … to list listname.
Remove … from list listname.
          and
Display listname as list.
Assign … to list listname.
```

In addition, you have learned several functions and methods that can be used with lists and the following functions, methods and new terms:

choice(…)	random( )	shuffle(…)
len(…)	randint(a,b)	.pop( )
.index(…)	.count(…)	.sort( )
lists	indexing	linked lists

Chapter 8
Basics of Program Design

With the exception of file I/O (saving data to and retrieving data from files,) you have now covered the basic operations involved in computer processing. You have all the different puzzle pieces you need to write useful computer programs. In this chapter, you will learn how to go about arranging these pieces into something that accomplishes a useful task.

The steps necessary for designing a successful program are outlined below as questions to be asked and, at least tentatively, answered before a single line of code is written.

Questions to Ask Before Writing One Line of Code

1. What is this program supposed to accomplish?
2. What information will the program need in order to bring about the desired output?
3. Where will this information come from?
4. What needs to be done with this information to bring about the desired outcomes?
5. How are these outcomes to be communicated to the real world, such as the end user?
6. Who will be involved with the program at steps 3, 4, and 5? (If appropriate, you should interview these people.

With the answers to these questions sketched out in your notebook, imagine you are the end-user. Walk yourself through that person's step-by-step interactions with your finished program and make notes about what you would like to see and what you would be expected to do. Jot down prompts and desired keyboard input and specific examples of output if appropriate. List the menus that might be needed and sketch out what they should include.

At this point, you will have identified several tasks that your program must carry out. Each of these will likely become a function in your program. You can begin writing a **skeleton program**, listing these functions, giving them appropriate names, and, in the Main Program, writing out the function calls in the order they will need to be executed. You may begin to see where conditional blocks and loops are needed. An example might look like this:

```
Comment: Skeleton Program Outline.
[Function greeting using ():
    Return "".
    End of function block.]

[Function main_menu using ():
    Comment: Loop here to validate response.
    Return "".
    End of function block.]

Comment: ******************.
Comment: Main Program Begins Here.
Call function greeting with () for XXX.
Call function main_menu with () for XXX.
Comment: Conditional branching here to.
Comment: selected functions from menu.
```

The skeleton should follow correct syntax so it can be run, although at this point nothing happens. Test it and correct

any errors. Now you can pick a function and write the code
for it, then set up the Main Program so that it can call that
function and test its code. An example based on the above
skeleton is shown in Demo8.1.

```
Comment: Demo8.1 for Program Development.
Comment: Skeleton Program Outline.
[Function greeting using ():
    Display "Hi! Please enter your name. ".
    Get string for username.
    Return username.
    End of function block.]

[Function main_menu using ():
    Comment: Loop here to validate response.
    Return "".
    End of function block.]

Comment: ******************.
Comment: Main Program Begins Here.
Call function greeting with () for username.
Display username.
Call function main_menu with () for XXX.
Comment: Conditional branching here to.
Comment: selected functions from menu.
```

Note that the Main Program has changed only slightly,
just enough to make the function call work and to test the
return value to verify that the function is doing its job.

Do this for each successive function in your program. In
this way you can systematically write and test one function
at a time.

You may have twenty different functions. The order in
which they appear above the main program doesn't matter.
But when you begin writing the function calls in the main

program, you can begin to see how the program must proceed to accomplish its goals. Of course, you will undoubtedly come up with a few more functions you hadn't thought of.

Within just a few hours, you will have made significant progress toward developing your program. The skeleton code is like the frame for a new house under construction. The bare 2x4 frame has been nailed in place. You can see the neighborhood beyond between the studs. But when you look at the frame, you can picture what the finished house will look like. The same is true for your skeleton program.

A Real-World Application
Tic-Tac-Toe for Two

For the remainder of this chapter, we will develop a Tic Tac Toe program for two people and convert the finished product into an executable file that can be run on any machine having the same operating system as yours.

Going through the list of questions for this simple game program, most of the answers are obvious. The program is to be an interactive game for two people to play tic-tac-toe. The program needs to assign each player, in turn, a token, either 'X' or 'O'. This information needs to be stored from one round to the next so an updated display of the grid can be presented for the players to see. Finally, after each turn, the grid needs to be evaluated to see if the most recent player has won the game, and if so, a 'You Won' message is presented. The game ends when this happens, or when all nine squares have been selected.

The paragraph above provides the general specifications for the program. Since KwicKode doesn't have access to sophisticated graphics, simple text graphics will have to be used, displaying one row of text at a time. Sketching out what we might want the players to see, we come up with the following sample:

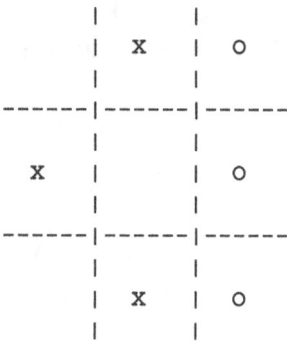

Only three of the eleven rows displayed contain data. Two strings will be sufficient for the remaining nine rows. We'll call them vert and horiz, as follows:

```
Assign "       |       |" to vert.
Assign "------|------|------" to horiz.
```

Now, if we have three lists, a, b, and c with three elements in each that are either a blank space, an 'X' or an 'O', these can be updated after each play and placed in their appropriate strings for the display. All eleven strings can be elements in a list called 'grid', and the entire grid can be displayed with:.

```
Display grid as list.
```

Of course, in the excitement of a new project, we're getting ahead of ourselves here. Best stop and flesh out the full skeleton of the program. How do we want the program to operate? Let's list the steps.

1.   Get the player's names and assign tokens. This looks like two linked lists with only two elements in each. Let's call them 'names' and 'tags'.

2.   Display the empty grid.

3.   Prompt a player to choose a cell for their token. Verify that the entry is a valid play (that is, an empty cell), otherwise repeat the prompt.

4.   When a valid response has been made, update the a, b, and c lists.

5.   Use the data in a, b, and c to create strings for grid[1], grid[5], and grid[9]. Display the new grid.

6.   Check to see if a 'three-in-a-row' has been established. If so, congratulate the winner and end the game.

7.   Otherwise, check to see if the grid has been filled. If so, announce a tie and end the game.

8.   If the game is still on-going, return to #3 for the other player's turn.

With this outline, we can create the skeleton for the program and sketch out the skeleton structures for the various functions we'll need.

```
Comment: Tic Tac Toe for Two Skeleton.
[Function get_players using (names):
    Return names.
    End of function block.]

[Function create_grid using (grid):
    Return grid.
    End of function block.]

[Function draw_grid using (grid,a,b,c):
    Return "".
    End of function block.]

[Function game_play using (grid, a,b,c):
Comment: Use 2 loops here for each round and each turn.
Comment: For each turn, call get_move, draw_grid,.
Comment and call chk_status.
    Return "".
    End of function block.]

[Function get_move using (name, tag, grid, a,b,c):
    Return grid.
    End of function block.]

[Function chk_status using (name, tag, grid, a,b,c):
    Return "".
    End of function block.]

Comment: Main Program.
Create list grid.
Create list names.
Create list tags.
Create list a.
Create list b.
Create list c.
Add "X", "O" to list tags.
Call function get_players with (names) for names.
Add " "," "," " to list a.
Add " "," "," " to list b.
Add " "," "," " to list c.
Call function create_grid with (grid) for grid.
Call function game_play using (grid,a,b,c) for Z.
```

As we work through the skeleton of the program, we realize that the 'database' we need can be achieved with three lists containing three 1-letter strings each, three for row A, three for row B and three for row C. These lists are then passed back and forth between the functions as a, b, and c. If this were the case, then it would fall to the draw_grid function to build the row to be displayed from the a, b, and c lists.

Having made that decision, we can flesh out the main program as shown above, creating the lists we need and filling all but the names list with the initial data. The main program then gets the players' names (#1), creates and displays the empty grid (#2), and turns the program over to the game_play function. The main program is finished.

Now let's look at each function one at a time. First up is the get_players function:

```
[Function get_players using (names):
  [Repeat block while cntr<2 with cntr:
    Display "Enter name for the "+tags[cntr]+" player: ".
    Get string for name.
    Add name to list names.
    End of repeat block.]
  Return names.
  End of function block.]
```

We have two names to get, so a two-cycle repeat block is used to get names and these are assigned 'X' or 'O' respectively since names and tags are linked lists. Note the use of the plural for list names and the singular when dealing with one element. This approach helps to keep things straight. Of course, the list name (plural) must be used when an index is attached, as in names[1].

The create_grid function fills the grid with the vert and horiz strings mentioned earlier. Create_grid is called only once at the start of each game. Since the database a, b, and c strings have blanks at the start (main program), the draw_grid function can also be used to draw the blank starting grid.

```
[Function create_grid using (grid):
   Assign "        |    |" to vert.
   Assign "    ---|---|---" to horiz.
   [Repeat block while k < 11 with k:
      Add vert to list grid.
      [If k==3 or k==7 then:
         Assign horiz to grid[k].
         End of if block.]
      End of repeat block.]
   Call function draw_grid with (grid) for grid.
   Display grid as list.
   Return grid.
   End of function block.]
```

Filling the eight unchanging grid rows only once at the start saves us from doing this every time the grid is displayed. After each play, the draw_grid function refreshes only the three playable rows. Note: After testing, it was decided to add row headers to make it easier for the players to select the cell they wish to play. Always keep your eyes peeled for ways to improve your programs beyond the initial design specifications.

```
[Function draw_grid using (grid, a,b,c):
   Assign "A.    "+a[0]+" | "+a[1]+" | "+a[2] to grid[1].
   Assign "B.    "+b[0]+" | "+b[1]+" | "+b[2] to grid[5].
   Assign "C.    "+c[0]+" | "+c[1]+" | "+c[2] to grid[9].
   Display "".
   Display grid as list.
   Display "".
   Return grid.
   End of function block.]
```

The game_play function handles the two nested loops required by the game. The inner loop has just two cycles corresponding to each player's turn. The outer loop cycles for each round of play. As with all loops, some flag must be set that determines when to end the loop. In this case, it is the variable 'game' set to 'GO' or 'STOP'. When 'GO', the outer loop continues to cycle. The inner loop cycles twice based on its loop counter, which is set equal to 2 if it is desired to end the loop early.

So this function extracts the current player's name and token and calls the 'get_move' function, and then the 'draw_grid' function. Finally, it calls the 'status' function to decide if the current player has won the game or if the game has ended in a tie. The loop ends by taking appropriate actions to end the loop if either someone has won or if the game has ended in a tie.

```
[Function game_play using (grid,a,b,c):
  Assign "GO" to game.
  [Repeat block while game=="GO" with round:
    [Repeat block while turn < 2  with turn:
        Call function get_move with (turn,a,b,c) for blank.
        Call function draw_grid with (grid,a,b,c) for grid.
        Call function status with (turn, a, b, c) for win.
        [If (win != "No" or round == 4) then:
            Assign "STOP" to game.
            Assign 2 to turn.
            End of if block.]
        End of repeat block.]
      End of repeat block.]
  [If win == "No" then:
    Display "TIE GAME.".
    Display "That was fun. Come again!".
    End of if block.]
  Return "".
  End of function block.]
```

When the 'get_move' function is called, it accepts the player's cell selection, verifies it is valid (looping back if it is not), and entering the appropriate token value into the database a, b, or c for the selected cell.

Recall that the 'Get string for...' command must be preceded by a 'Display...' prompt that contains a single string. For multiple elements, the single string requirement can be met by concatenating several strings together.

A useful technique is employed here. The value entered, entry, is a two-character string, such as 'B2'. To be useful, it must be split into 'B' and the number '2' (using the int(...) function) so that the token can be placed correctly into the a, b, c database lists. Both KwicKode and Python treat strings as a special case of lists, with each letter being indexed sequentially (from zero, of course). So 'entry[0]' contains the row letter and 'entry[1]' contains the column number. Thus the required data can be extracted from the keyboard entry.

With this information, the selected cell is checked to be sure it is still empty. If it is, the a,b,c database is updated and the loop ends with assigning 'legal' to the move_ok variable controlling the loop.

```
[Function get_move using (idx, a, b, c ):
  Assign names[idx] to name.
  Assign tags[idx] to tag.
  Assign "illegal" to move_ok.
  [Repeat block while move_ok == "illegal" with cntr:
    Display name+", enter cell (eg. A1) for your "+tag+":".
    Get string for entry.
    Assign entry[0].upper() to row.
    Assign int(entry[1])-1 to col.
    [If (row == "A" and a[col] == " ") then:
```

```
         Assign tag to a[col].
         Assign "legal" to move_ok.
         End of if block.]
    [If (row == "B" and b[col] == " ") then:
         Assign tag to b[col].
         Assign "legal" to move_ok.
         End of if block.]
    [If (row == "C" and c[col] == " ") then:
         Assign tag to c[col].
         Assign "legal" to move_ok.
         End of if block.]
     End of repeat block.]
   Return "".
   End of function block.]
```

Finally, we come to the 'status' function which analyzes the database to determine if the current player's token appears 3-in-a-row, 3-in-a-column, or 3-in-a-diagonal. For the three rows, the '.count()' method makes finding 3 tokens easy. For the columns, a repeat loop using the counter 'cnt' for index control is used, and for the diagonals, the three relevant cells in each is checked in a single conditional statement.

```
[Function status using (idx, a, b, c):
   Assign names[idx] to name.
   Assign tags[idx] to tag.
   Assign a.count(tag) to acntr.
   Assign b.count(tag) to bcntr.
   Assign c.count(tag) to ccntr.
   Assign "No" to win.
   [If (acntr==3 or bcntr==3 or ccntr==3) then:
     Assign "WON!" to win.
     End of if block.]
   [Repeat block while cnt < 3 with cnt:
     [If (a[cnt]==tag and b[cnt]== tag and c[cnt]==tag) then:
         Assign " WON!" to win.
```

```
      End of if block.]
    End of repeat block.]
  [If (a[0]==tag and b[1]==tag and c[2]==tag) then:
    Assign " WON!" to win.
    End of if block.]
  [If (a[2]==tag and b[1]==tag and c[0]==tag) then:
    Assign " WON!" to win.
    End of if block.]
  [If win != "No" then:
    Display name + " WON!".
    End of if block.]
  Return win.
  End of function block.]
```

With that detailed analysis, all the parts and pieces are put together below showing the full 133-line program.

Tic-Tac-Toe for Two with Text Graphics

```
Comment: Demo8.2 Tic Tac Toe.
Comment: by Bishop, 2/7/2025.

[Function get_players using (names):
  [Repeat block while cntr<2 with cntr:
    Display "Enter name for the "+tags[cntr]+" player: "
    Get string for name.
    Add name to list names.
    End of repeat block.]
  Return names.
  End of function block.]

[Function create_grid using (grid):
  Assign "        |     |" to vert.
  Assign "     ---|---|---" to horiz.
  [Repeat block while k < 11 with k:
    Add vert to list grid.
    [If k==3 or k==7 then:
```

```
                Assign horiz to grid[k].
                End of if block.]
          [Else:
             [If k==1 then:
                Assign "A." + grid[k][2:] to grid[k].
                End of if block.]
             [If k==5 then:
                Assign "B." + grid[k][2:] to grid[k].
                End of if block.]
             [If k==9 then:
                Assign "C." + grid[k][2:] to grid[k].
                End of if block.]
             End of else block.]
          End of repeat block.]
       Display grid as list.
       Return grid.
       End of function block.]

[Function draw_grid using (grid, a,b,c):
    Assign "A.    "+a[0]+" | "+a[1]+" | "+a[2] to grid[1].
    Assign "B.    "+b[0]+" | "+b[1]+" | "+b[2] to grid[5].
    Assign "C.    "+c[0]+" | "+c[1]+" | "+c[2] to grid[9].
    Display "".
    Display grid as list.
    Display "".
    Return grid.
    End of function block.]

[Function game_play using (grid,a,b,c):
   Assign "GO" to game.
   [Repeat block while game=="GO" with round:
     [Repeat block while turn < 2  with turn:
        Call function get_move with (turn,a,b,c) for blank.
        Call function draw_grid with (grid,a,b,c) for grid.
        Call function status with (turn, a, b, c) for win.
        [If (win != "no" or round == 4) then:
             Assign "STOP" to game.
             Assign 2 to turn.
             End of if block.]
          End of repeat block.]
       End of repeat block.]
```

```
   [If win == "no" then:
      Display "TIE GAME.".
      Display "That was fun. Come again!".
      End of if block.]
   Return "".
   End of function block.]


[Function get_move using (idx, a, b, c ):
   Assign names[idx] to name.
   Assign tags[idx] to tag.
   Assign "illegal" to move_ok.
   [Repeat block while move_ok == "illegal" with cntr:
      Display name+", enter cell (eg. A1) for your "+tag+":".
      Get string for entry.
      Assign entry[0].upper() to row.
      Assign int(entry[1])-1 to col.
      [If (row == "A" and a[col] == " ") then:
         Assign tag to a[col].
         Assign "legal" to move_ok.
         End of if block.]
      [If (row == "B" and b[col] == " ") then:
         Assign tag to b[col].
         Assign "legal" to move_ok.
         End of if block.]
      [If (row == "C" and c[col] == " ") then:
         Assign tag to c[col].
         Assign "legal" to move_ok.
         End of if block.]
      End of repeat block.]
    Return "".
   End of function block.]
[Function status using (idx, a, b, c):
   Assign names[idx] to name.
   Assign tags[idx] to tag.
   Assign a.count(tag) to acntr.
   Assign b.count(tag) to bcntr.
   Assign c.count(tag) to ccntr.
   Assign "no" to win.
   [If (acntr==3 or bcntr==3 or ccntr==3) then:
```

```
     Assign "WON!" to win.
   End of if block.]
[Repeat block while cnt < 3 with cnt:
   [If (a[cnt]==tag and b[cnt]==tag and c[cnt]==tag) then:
      Assign " WON!" to win.
      End of if block.]
   End of repeat block.]
[If (a[0]==tag and b[1]==tag and c[2]==tag) then:
   Assign " WON!" to win.
   End of if block.]
[If (a[2]==tag and b[1]==tag and c[0]==tag) then:
   Assign " WON!" to win.
   End of if block.]
[If win != "no" then:
   Display name + " WON!".
   End of if block.]
Return win.
End of function block.]


Comment: ******************.
Comment: Main Program.
Create list grid.
Create list names.
Create list tags.
Create list a.
Create list b.
Create list c.
Add "X", "O" to list tags.
Call function get_players with (names) for names.
Add " "," "," " to list a.
Add " "," "," " to list b.
Add " "," "," " to list c.
Call function create_grid with (grid) for grid.
Call function game_play with (grid,a,b,c) for Z.
```

Creating an Executable File

Till now, all of the programs you have written as .txt files and compiled to .py files have been totally confined to your personal computer and to the Python directory where your python environment resides. But the whole point of creating new programs is sharing them with the world (or at least your best friends.) Not everyone (Mom and Dad, for example) has a Python directory on their computer.

If you have developed an application for an office environment, you don't want your code to be tampered with by a curious (or malevolent) employee. The first step in making your code bulletproof is to turn your Python version into an executable file.

This section describes how to convert .py program files into **.exe executables.** Once you have an .exe version of a program, you can email it to anyone who has the same operating system as yours and they will be able to run it and enjoy the results of your efforts. But the program will remain safe from tampering.

The program that performs this conversion is pyinstaller. To load this program, first open a terminal window as follows:

In Windows: <Windows-R> and enter 'cmd'.
In macOS: <Command-Space> and enter 'Terminal'.
In Ubuntu: <Ctrl-Alt-T>.

Enter the following command directly after the prompt.

pip install pyinstaller

Once the program has installed, if your program is named 'battleship.py', enter the following:

pyinstaller –onefile battleship.py

It's likely that the installer will object that it can't find your file, telling you it doesn't exist. Actually, it just doesn't know where to look. But the error message may give you the exact path needed, for example, in Windows terminal::

C:\Users\yourname\AppData\Local\Programs\Python\Python312

So, highlight this path and <Ctrl-C> to copy it, then retype the previous command, pasting in the path, followed by '\' and your program name, as in:

pyinstaller –onefile C:\Users\yourname\AppData\Local\
Programs\Python\Python312\battleship.py

This should satisfy the installer. You may have to search for your executable file. In Windows, it will be found in

C:\Users\yourname\dist\battleship.exe

Put a copy on your desktop. Double-click the icon and Voila! Your battleship program is up and running. You are ready to dazzle the world with your creation!

Note: This process will also work for any text-based Python application you may create in the future. But, as described here, the specific commands work only with

Windows operating systems. To create executables for other operating systems, you must build a 'virtual machine' on your computer that runs other operating systems. Set up Python there, enter the Python version of your program, and create an executable specifically for that operating system. Details are beyond the scope of this manual.

An excellent exercise for this chapter is to modify the tic-tac-toe program to make it more functional. Add a loop in the main program that allows the players to play multiple games. Include a linked list for each player's wins and display a scoreboard after each game and an option to continue playing or to quit.

Next, modify the game to allow the option of having two players or one player vs. the computer. For this second option, when it's the computer's turn, scan through the cells for an empty cell and have the computer choose it for its play. Of course, this game will be easy for the user to win, but wait. There's more.

Finally, when playing against the computer, add a function in which the computer makes informed decisions to determine which cell to choose. For example, if 3-in-a-row is available, then that cell is chosen and the computer wins. Second, if the opponent has two-in-a-row, then the cell to choose is the one that blocks the opponent

In this lesson you have learned how to put together specifications for a programming project, how to create a skeleton outline for a program, and how to flesh out the skeleton to create a functioning program. You have also learned how to convert your .py Python programs into executables that can be run outside of your Python programming environment.

skeleton program   .exe executable files

Chapter 9
File I/O

To round out KwicKode's functionality, only the commands for file I/O remain, using either **.txt (text)** or **.csv (comma separated variables)** file formats. Fortunately, in KwicKode, these are easy to understand and implement.

KwicKode requires a file name to have either a '.txt' or '.csv' suffix, as in 'membership.csv'. This tells the translator that the name represents a file and which file format to use. Because of this, parameter names cannot be substituted for file names in functions (unlike Python.)

As for deciding which file type to use, make your choice based on whether the data being saved is a block of text (as in a will or a sales document) that will be viewed or edited in a word processing program. If so, choose the .txt format. For lists of separate objects (like friends' email addresses or pet names or member records in a database) use the.csv format. This format is common to spreadsheet programs.

In the previous chapter, you saw how multiple linked lists (like a player's name and game tag) can be used to create a simple database. But without file storage capabilities, those lists have little value. Every time you turn off the computer, the lists disappear! File I/O opens the door to the real world of computer processing.

The first step for using files is to create a file with the 'Create file...' command. If the file already exists, this command will empty it of any previous data, creating an empty file. You encountered this behavior before with the 'Create list...' command.

```
Create file my_assets.csv.
Create file my_will.txt.
```

Once a file has been created, an entire list can be stored in the file. If it is a .csv file, the comma separated format in the list is maintained in the file. If the file is a .txt file, the entire text is saved in the file as one long string unless each line is a separate entry in the list. This, of course, is how you would want your document displayed.

The last of the KwicKode commands controls both file input and output. The first example below is a 'save' operation with data going out to the file to be saved. The second is a 'retrieve' operation with data being transferred from the file back into the list for your program to use. The translator knows which operation to perform by the order in which the two variables appear.

```
Copy data from portfolio to my_assets.csv.
Copy data from my_assets.csv to portfolio.
```

(Note: The word 'database' replaces the word 'data' when the file is to store a 'list of records'. See Chapter 12.)

The names you use for your files do not have to match the names of the lists. If the 'Create file...' command is not used between successive saves, each save operation appends the current list to the old. If the current list contains the old information, this will cause unwanted duplication of information in the file.

So, saving data to be used tomorrow, or next week, or next year, is simply a matter of putting the data in one or more lists (if it is not already a list), and then copying each list to corresponding data files. This creates a database where your information is archived for future use.

Demo9.1 demonstrates file I/O commands for a .csv file. It's interesting to note that the Python version of this program requires 50 lines of code vs. KwicKode's 14 lines.

```
Comment: Demo9.1 File I/O with .csv.
Comment:  by Bishop 1/20/25.
Create list my_friends.
Add "Annie","Billy","Carol" to list my_friends.
Display "My friends before saving: ".
Display my_friends as list.
Create file friends.csv.
Copy data from my_friends to friends.csv.
Create list my_friends.
Display "I emptied the list of my friends: ".
Display my_friends.
Display "Now I will retrieve the data from the".
Display "file and restore the list. ".
Copy data from friends.csv to my_friends.
Display my_friends as list.
```

Run the Demo9.1 program. Then close the Python program window and add the word 'Comment:' in front of the 'Create file...' line in your KwicKode file, effectively removing that line. Save and compile the result, then run the program again and note the results. As you can see, if you don't empty the file with a 'Create file...' command, contents will continue to be duplicated.

On the other hand, when retrieving all the data from a file to a list, you would always want to dump it into an empty list. With that in mind, KwicKode automatically creates the empty list for you as part of the data retrieval process.

For large blocks of text, you will want to save your manuscript in a .txt file. That way, other applications designed for text (like Word or Notepad) can readily read your files. A word of caution here, though. Look at the quotation marks in the code below. They are straight 'up-and-down' marks, not smart quotes or curly quotes. The Python interpreter will crash every time it runs into a curly quote. So, if you edit your .txt KwicKode programs in anything other than IDLE, take pains to be sure your quotation marks are acceptable. When you copy such a program text into IDLE prior to compiling it, you may have to retype all of the double and single quote symbols (and hyphens too) to satisfy the Python interpreter.

With Demo9.2 where a text file is involved, your block of text is entered and saved one line at a time into a list. That way, when the text is retrieved from the .txt file, when you use the 'as list' option with the 'Display...' command, your text will be displayed as expected.

```
Comment: Demo9.2 Manuscript text in .txt file.
Comment: by Bishop, 1/27/25.
[Function show_and_tell using (my_book):
    Display "Here is your work so far: ".
    Display my_book as list.
    Return "".
    End of function block.]
```

```
[Function get_info using (my_book):
   Display "********************************".
   Display "Enter manuscript one line at a time.".
   Display "Enter 0 to quit.".
   Assign "" to entry.
   [Repeat block while entry != "0" with idx:
       Display "Next line...".
       Get string for entry.
       [If entry != "0" then:
           Add entry to list my_book.
           End of if block.]
       End of repeat block.]
   Return "".
   End of function block.]

[Function retrieve_data using (my_book):
   Display "Is this an existing file? (Y/N) ".
   Get string for ans.
   [If ans.upper() == "N" then:
      Create file my_book.txt.
      End of if block.]
   [Else:
      Copy data from my_book.txt to my_book.
      End of if block.]
   Return my_book.
   End of function block.]

[Function save_data using (my_book):
   Display "Your manuscript will now be saved.".
   Create file my_book.txt.
   Copy data from my_book to my_book.txt.
   Return "".
   End of function block.]
Comment: ***************************.
Comment: Main program.
Create list my_book.
Call function retrieve_data with (my_book) for my_book.
Call function show_and_tell with (my_book) for blank.
Call function get_info with (my_book) for blank.
Call function show_and_tell with (my_book) for blank.
Call function save_data with (my_book) for blank.
```

Each successive run of demo9.2 will allow you to add more lines to the datafile and flesh out the manuscript. If you merely want to see it, run the program and enter '0' to quit, resulting in the full text being displayed.

Printed Output

Related to file I/O for KwicKode is obtaining printed output when it is necessary to display the contents of your database on reconstituted trees. KwicKode does not have a separate 'Print...' command, but that doesn't mean that print output is unavailable.

The key is that your database files are either .txt or .csv files. Any word processor can open the .txt files, and you can then choose to print the file from that application. This mode also gives you the opportunity to fine-tune the output with bold or colored print, underlining, and varying font sizes.

As for the .csv files, most spreadsheet programs, such as Excel, are geared specifically toward this format. Open your database .csv file with a spreadsheet program. You will see your data spread out in separate columns and rows in the spreadsheet. As with the .txt file, you can then use the spreadsheet program to tweak your output to fit your needs before printing it. This works especially well when you wish to print only part of your database. In the spreadsheet, you can highlight only what you want printed and then choose "print selection" from the application's print menu.

This method also works if you have developed a database program with a list of email addresses that you might wish to use for a bulk email or physical addresses for a bulk mail project. Load your .csv file into a spreadsheet program, highlight the email address column, and copy/paste the addresses into the 'blind carbon copy' field of your email program.

This process works in reverse as well. Many important governmental and research organizations maintain online databases for a wide variety of topics (e.g. NOAA weather information; Census Bureau data). Usually, that data is available for download in .csv formats. You can use the KwicKode 'Copy…' command to load these files into your own KwicKode database program (Chapter 12) designed for that particular set of data and have total control, through your program code, to research the information provided.

Next up, the vast field of database science will be introduced, with examples in KwicKode that demonstrate how to use linked lists for simple databases. Then, in Chapters 12 and 13, two full-fledged database programs using a list of records are shown. The first illustrates data archiving in a static database, while the second demonstrates a dynamic database useful for keeping an organization's membership records, for a store's inventory control, or for a personal portfolio management system. The possibilities are limited only by your imagination.

You now have learned all of KwicKode's commands and how to use them. You have the coding tools at your disposal to tackle a great many real-world applications. Even better, you know how to tailer these programs to suit your particular needs. The world is at your fingertips!

Rework the last program exercise from Chapter 7 so that after each addition or deletion from the list, the list is saved as a .csv file, then retrieved and displayed after the line: 'Display "This is the list that was retrieved:" Of course, this list and the one previously displayed after the add or remove operation, should be identical.

In this lesson you have learned how to create .txt and .csv files for storing data, and how to save and retrieve data from these files. You learned that the files only accept and return data in lists and that file names must end in either .txt or .csv suffixes in KwicKode.

```
Create file filename.
Copy data from listname to filename.
Copy data from filename to listname.
```

In addition, you have learned several terms associated with file I/O.

file I/O   text files (.txt)
comma-separated values (.csv)

Chapter 10
Linked Lists and Databases

Demo program 7.3 used the 'Add ... to list' command to create two lists in which the data in one list (pets names) was related to the data in the other list (pet type). Similarly, Tic-Tac-Toe for Two saved the players' names and tokens in two separate but related lists. This type of synchronization in two or more lists is referred to as **linked lists**. Using linked lists is one way to create a simple database.

When using linked lists, keeping the objects synchronized in all the lists is of paramount importance. If the fourth object in list #1 is removed, then the fourth object in each of the linked lists must also be removed. If an object is added to one of the lists, then its corresponding related objects must be added to each of the other lists, even if that means adding a blank field. Thus, with linked lists, there is a lot of repetitive code, which is why you should consider them only when just a few lists are needed. Also, when you hear 'repetitive code' you should always think 'FUNCTIONS'.

Demo 10.1 creates a simple email address database for a book club roster. In this case, the lists are initially blank. They are filled with the 'Add ... to list ...' command. As with any database program, there is a menu function with a variety of options from which the user may choose. Each option leads to a separate function that contains the code to handle that activity.

```
Comment: Demo10.1 Linked List Database.

[Function get_memberlist using (members,emails):
   Copy data from scifimembers.csv to members.
   Copy data from scifiemails.csv to emails.
   Return members,emails.
   End of function block.]

[Function save_memberlist using (member,emails):
   Create file scifimembers.csv.
   Copy data from members to scifimembers.csv.
   Create file scifiemails.csv.
   Copy data from emails to scifiemails.csv.
   Return "".
   End of function block.]

[Function menu using ():
    Assign 0 to choice.
   [Repeat block while choice != 5 with cntr:
       Display "*"*30.
       Display "SciFi & Adventure Book Club".
       Display "Main MENU".
       Display "1. Add name. 2. Delete name. ".
       Display "3. Search. 4.Show list. 5. Quit. ".
       Get string for choice.
       Display "*"*30.
       [If choice not in ("12345") then:
          Display "Invalid entry. Try again. ".
          End of if block.]
       [Else:
          Assign int(choice) to choice.
          End of else block.]
       [If choice == 1 then:
           Call function new_member with () for Z.
           End of if block.]
       [If choice == 2 then:
           Call function remove_member with () for Z.
```

```
                End of if block.]
        [If choice == 3 then:
            Call function find_member with () for Z.
            End of if block.]
        [If choice == 4 then:
            Call function show_all with () for Z.
            End of if block.]
        End of while block.]
    Return "".
    End of function block.]

[Function new_member using ():
    Display "Enter new member's name. ".
    Get string for name.
    Display "Enter email address. ".
    Get string for email.
    Add name to list members.
    Add email to list emails.
    Return "".
    End of function block.]

[Function remove_member using ():
    Display "Who do you want to delete? ".
    Get string for name.
    Call function get_index with (name) for idx.
    [If idx != -1 then:
        Remove members[idx] from list members.
        Remove emails[idx] from list emails.
        Display name, "has been deleted. ".
        End of if block.]
    Return "".
    End of function block.]

[Function get_index using (name):
    [If members.count(name) != 0 then:
        Assign members.index(name) to idx.
        End of if block.]
    [Else:
        Display name, " is not a member. ".
        Assign -1 to idx.
```

```
          End of else block.]
      Return idx.
      End of function block.]

[Function find_member using ():
    Display "Who do you want to find? ".
    Get string for name.
    Call function get_index with (name) for idx.
    [If idx != -1 then:
        Display members[idx], ": ",emails[idx].
        End of if block.]
    Return "".
    End of function block.]

[Function show_all using ():
    Display "SciFi Book Club Members".
    Display "*"*20.
    [Repeat block while idx<len(members) with idx:
        Assign members[idx]+": "+emails[idx] to msg.
        Display (idx+1), ". ", msg.
        End of repeat block.]
    Return "".
    End of function block.]

Comment: ********************.
Comment: Main Program.
Create list members.
Create list emails.
Call function get_memberlist with (members,emails) for (members,emails).
Call function menu with () for blank.
Call function save_memberlist with (members,emails) for Z.
Display "End of Program. ".
Display "Good-Bye. ".
```

Many applications, including database programs, require the user to select from a menu that includes several actions. Menus are typically written as a function that is called early on by the main program and are part of a loop so that when one action is completed, the menu reappears. In this program, once the lists are set up and populated in the main program, the menu function is called.

In addition to displaying the options available and obtaining the user's selection, the menu must verify that the selection is valid. Then, as part of the loop, a series of conditional statements is used to branch the computer's operations to the functions appropriate for the selection. Once these are taken care of, the menu routine loops back to display the list of options again. This continues until the user decides to quit the program.

The loop controlling all this can be in the main program or in the menu function, in which case the main program is reduced to just a few lines of code. That is the case with Demo 10.1.

At the very least, database programs require functions for adding new data and displaying the data already collected, as well as retrieving data from the archives and storing the new data to a file. For static databases, such as data collection routines (Demo 12.1), this is all that is needed. But for applications in which previously entered data must be edited, searched, or removed, additional functions must be included to handle these actions. Demo 12.2 contains all of these functions.

As described in Chapter 7, using the '.index(...)' method works fine for finding data in your list provided all the names are unique. That is the search technique used in this program. Here's an example you might run into in searching for a particular member's data in a linked-list database for your club.

```
Display "Whose index number do you want to find?".
Get string for member_name.
Assign (club_members.index(member_name)) to indx.
```

However, if member_name isn't in the list, the Python interpreter will crash the program. So in Demo 12.1, the '.count(...)' method is used to ensure that the object being searched for does exist before the '.index(...)' method is employed. For cases where the name may not be unique, a loop should be used instead, with each successful match being displayed to give the user the option to continue the search or to settle on the record currently displayed.

Demo 12.1 contains each of these options in separate functions. To review: The program shows how to create a new, empty list, retrieve items stored in a .csv file, add items to the list, delete items from the list, and find a specific item in the list using the '.index(...)' method. It uses the 'len(...)' function for loop control, and the '.count(...)' method to verify that an object is in the list. Since index numbers begin at zero, 1 is added to the index number whenever it is used for display purposes do users don't have to deal with 'zero'.

For the menu, the '[If ... then:' statements take care of all allowed entries so everything else is ignored and the loop recycles back to the menu. However, in the search function, not finding a match could cause the program to crash, so the '.count(...)' method catches this possibility and, if it returns a zero, a message is displayed and the program continues.

As demonstrated by the 'display_item' function, referencing any particular item in a list can be done by attaching that item's index number in square brackets immediately after the variable name. Thus club_members[0] will access the first entry in the my_friends list, and with a linked list database, addresses[0], phone[0], and email[0] will reference that person's address, phone and email.

```
Display "Enter member name to retrieve address.".
Get string for member.
Assign club_members.count(member) to cnt.
[If cnt != 0 then:
    Assign (club_members.index(member)) to indx.
    Display member,"lives at", addresses[indx].
    End of if block.]
[Else:
    Display member,"is not in your database.".
    End of else block.]
```

To reiterate, once you have the person's index number from one list, you can use it with other lists to locate their addresses, phone numbers, etc. as in the sixth line above.

A more elegant approach to a database is to store all of a member's information in one list. This works because KwicKode (and Python) allows data of mixed types to share a list. With all of one member's data in one list, or '**record**', that whole list can be one element in a 'mother list', perhaps a 'members_database' list, giving you a list of lists (a list of records). Knowing the index number for a desired object allows you to retrieve the whole record from the database at once.

The two programs in Chapter 12 both use this approach. While the method of data storage is different from linked lists, much of the code in this chapter's program above will be duplicated in Chapter 12's programs with minor alterations to make them work in the more robust database environment.

For this chapter's exercise, modify the program code in Demo10.1 to create a pair of linked lists that contain data of interest to you, such as a song title and the artists name or a stock name and its symbol or price (or both…three linked lists).

Here is a list of the Python functions and methods that you can use in expressions as demonstrated in the above programs (sort, pop, and reverse have no parameters):

Functions: len(…)   sum(…)   max(…)
                min(…)
Methods: .count(…)   .index(…)   .sort( )
                .reverse( )   .pop( )

Chapter 11
Generalizing Functions

Previous chapters have included programs that include menus from which the user is asked to choose an option. The program in Chapter 10 provided a full function, 'menu', that presented options typical for database management. Part of that code is shown below.

```
[Function menu using ():
    Assign 0 to choice.
    [Repeat block while choice != 5 with cntr:
        Display "*"*30.
        Display "SciFi & Adventure Book Club".
        Display "Main MENU".
        Display "1. Add name. 2. Delete name. ".
        Display "3. Search. 4.Show list. 5. Quit. ".
        Get string for choice.
        Display "*"*30.
        [If choice not in ("12345") then:
            Display "Invalid entry. Try again. ".
            End of if block.]
        [Else:
            Assign int(choice) to choice.
            End of else block.]
```

As pointed out in Chapter 9, without an option to save the data entered to a file and retrieve it at some later date, that program fails to be a database program. The linked list database automatically retrieved the data at the start and saved it at the end. But usually one or both of these operations are included in the menu list of options.

Another function missing is the option to edit data previously entered. A 'sort' function might be useful and is common in database programs.

Add these four options to the five already listed in the menu, and you can begin to see how quickly something as simple as a program menu can grow. This is typical of many aspects of programming projects!

Also note that the menu function displays the list of choices in a loop. Inside the loop, after the user enters their selection, a validation process checks to make sure the selection is valid. If it isn't, an error message is displayed and the loop repeats itself. The chart below depicts the activities required of a menu function.

1. Display a title for the menu.
2. Display the menu options.
3. Prompt the user to enter a choice.
4. Get input from the keyboard.
5. Validate the input, cycling back to 2 or 3 if invalid.
6. Return the choice to the function call.

All menus will follow this general outline. But every application's menu will be unique. The title and menu choices for a book club membership list will be different from that of an inventory or checkbook register application.

But wait! With careful use of lists and function parameters, we ought to be able to write code for a menu function that could be used for virtually any application. If we do this, that code can simply be pasted into all applications that need a menu. We'll never have to write code for a menu again! This is the idea behind **generalizing functions** and provides the foundation for program modules.

In this chapter, we'll create a generalized menu function. We'll also see how generalizing techniques can be applied to several other database operations. Always be thinking about ways to generalize your code so its usefulness extends beyond the scope of the immediate project.

Generalizing the Menu Function

In Chapter 10, the menu function also includes the conditional branching statements that accompany each of the menu options. Different applications may have different names for the functions called by these conditional statements, which would negate the generalization process, so our first decision is to not include those in the generalized menu. The menu function will simply use 'Return' to send the validated selection back to the function call and let some other function, or the main program itself, handle the conditional branching.

Item 1 in the chart above is very easy to generalize. Using the variable name 'dbname' as a parameter in the function's parameter list, the following line works for all applications:

```
[Function db_menu using (dbname):
    Display "Database "+dbname+" Menu: ".
```

Prior to the function call, the actual name to be used is assigned to a variable that the call can use in its argument list. For example:

```
Assign "SciFi & Adventure Book Club" to club_name.
Call function db_menu with (club_name) for selection.
```

Next, we look at the nine menu options identified at the beginning of this chapter. If we put them into a list called 'options', then 'options' can be included alongside 'club_name' in the call's argument list and a corresponding parameter can be named to accept the list for the function's use.

```
Assign "SciFi & Adventure Book Club" to club_name.
Assign "Add name","Delete name","Edit record" to list options.
Add "Search","View list", "Quit Program" to list options.
Assign "ADESVQ" to codes.
Call function db_menu with (club_name, options, codes) for
          selection.
```

Note that the option descriptions and the keyboard codes have been separated. The reason for this becomes apparent when we see how the validation sequence works, essentially treating these two as linked lists. The full generalized menu function is show below. Within this code, there is only one non-generic feature. Can you find it?

Note also the use of the len(…) function attached to the repeat block that displays the options. This further generalizes the code, in that now we can use the menu regardless of the number of options we decide to present. Five options? Ten options? The code will still work.

Here, then, is a block of code that can be pasted into dozens of programs with little or no alteration.

```
[Function db_menu using (db_name, options, choices):
    Display "Database "+db_name+" Main Menu: ".
    Assign "X" to choice.
    [Repeat block while choice not in choices with z:
        [Repeat block while cnt < len(choices) with cnt:
            Display choices[cnt]+ " - "+options[cnt].
            End of repeat block.]
        Display "Enter your selection... ".
        Get string for choice.
        Assign choice.upper() to choice.
        [If choice not in choices then:
            Display "Not a valid choice. Try again.".
            End of if block.]
        End of repeat block.]
    Return choice.
    End of function block.]
```

To demonstrate the utility of generalized functions, this menu will be used as is for the dynamic database example in the second half of Chapter 12. That program also shows how creative use of lists for repeating elements in database functions (field names, for example) can also be used to generalize functions. This is the subject of the next section.

Using Lists to Generalize Functions

One thing databases have in common is lists. Lists, lists, and more lists. In fact, the database itself is one giant list when you come to think about it. But lists also make it easy to generalize many functions that are common to all databases besides the menu function describe above.

For example, each record in a list is composed of several fields, such as 'First Name', 'Last Name', 'Address', 'City', 'State', 'Zip Code', 'Phone', etc. Or, for an inventory database: 'Item', 'Quantity', 'Source', 'Price', etc. Now think of the functions that display records, add records, edit records, and sort records. All of these functions need the above information to label the items being displayed or to label the blank lines to be filled out.

Now if a list called 'field_list' is created in the main program and filled with the field labels appropriate to that application, it can be used in each of the function calls mentioned above just like the options list in the generalized menu function. Each function will have a corresponding variable, say 'fields', to accept the data. Within the function itself, a loop like the one used within db_menu displays these field names in whatever format is appropriate for the given function. For example:

```
Assign "Item","Quantity","Source","Cost","Price" to list field_list.
```

The function call can add 'field_list' as one of the arguments to be passed to the sort function:

```
Call function sort with (inv_name, field_list) for z.
```

The function's first lines may then look like this:

```
[Function sort using (dbname, fields):
    Assign -1 to choice.
    Display "Sorting function for ", dbname, "database. ".
    [Repeat block while choice != len(fields) with z.
        [Repeat block while cnt < len(fields) with cnt.
            Display cnt+" - " + fields[cnt].
            End of repeat block.]
```

```
Display cnt+" - " + "Return to Main Menu. "
Display "Enter the number for the field to be used, ".
Display "or 0 to return. ".
Get string for sort_field.
Assign int(sort_field) to sort_field.
[If not (sortfield>=0 and sortfield<len(fields)) the
    Display "Not a valid choice. Try again. ".
    End of if block.]
End of repeat block.]
etc., etc.
```

Notice the totally generic nature of the code in the sort function. The code could be used without alteration in hundreds of applications. It works with field lists of any length. Yet each application would have its own unique appearance with the field names applicable to its own database being displayed.

Also note the striking similarities between this code example and the generalized db_menu function. The user is given a list of fields from which to choose, and the choice must be validated.

As an exercise, write a complete generic 'add_record' function for a database with at least six fields. Each field name will be displayed in a prompt for a 'Get string' that will accept user input for the value to be associated with that field name. Also write the Assign statement for the field list for your example, and the function call, as shown above.

In this chapter you have learned about the advantages of generalizing code that appears in functions and seen a few examples of how that is accomplished. The key is choosing parameter variables and list variables that can be used within their respective functions without having any reference to the actual values they represent.

Chapter 12
Database as a List of Records

Static Databases

Chapter 10 presented the linked list method for maintaining a simple database with only two or three elements per record. This works for a membership email list, but most real-world databases include far more than two or three items per record. Maintaining synchronized lists across a dozen or more items can be a daunting task.

Fortunately, there is a better solution, and that is to allocate all the data pertaining to a single entity (a member or an inventory item) to its own list. This works because both KwicKode and Python allow elements of different types to reside in the same list. Now if your club has 150 members, you can create a single list called 'membership' that contains 150 lists within it, with each of these 'sub-lists', or **records**, corresponding to a single member's data.

This 'list of lists', or 'list of records', requires two index numbers to identify or access any single piece of information. The first index number relates to the outer 'membership' list. So, 'Display membership[5].' will show all of the sixth member's data at once because the data is contained in its own list. The second index number refers to the specific item within that member's record. 'Display membership[5][0].'

will only display the sixth member's name, assuming that the member's name is the first item in the record.

It is important to note that the ordering of specific elements in the record must be defined at the outset and maintained rigidly, even if it requires entering blank information for missing items. If the sixth element is a phone number for one member, the sixth element for all members must be their phone numbers.

Another requirement is that you must use the .csv format for your database file and you can't substitute a parameter name for the file name in functions. (Python does allow this.) The reason for this is that the translator program specifically looks for the .csv suffix as it converts your KwicKode file into Python code.

There is one variation in the KwicKode commands you need to use for saving and retrieving data in a list-of-records. In the 'Copy…' command, you must substitute the word 'database' for the word 'data'. Using this keyword signals to the kk_to_py_translator.py program that you are using a list of records. So, the output and input commands might look like the following.

```
Copy database from friends_list to friends.csv.
Copy database from friends.csv to friends_list.
```

In many cases, once the information is stored in a database, it never needs changing. These are **static,** or **archival** databases. Data-collection operations fall into this category. Demo12.1 illustrates how a program might be designed for this purpose. This program maintains a database file on the local weather. The user enters a date, temperature, and precipitation amount, and that data is saved forever as a single record in the file precip.csv, never to be edited or deleted from the file.

Since the programs in this chapter are much longer than those you've encountered before, each function and the main program are presented separately with comments, starting with the main program (which, of course, must appear last).

The Daily Precipitation Database Program

The Main Program:

```
Comment:  "*********************************".
Comment:  "   Main Program Begins Here.
Assign "="*32 to zip.
Create list precip.
Create list fields.
Create list formats.
Add "Date (mm/dd/yy)","Temp.(C)","Precip.(cm)" to list fields.
Add "18C","10C","12C" to list formats.
Call function get_data with (precip) for precip.
Call function show_data with (precip, 10) for Z.
Display zip.
Display "Data Entry Routine for New Data.".
Display zip.
Call function get_new with (precip) for precip.
Display zip.
Call function show_data with (precip, 10) for Z.
Display "Saving data and leaving program.".
Call function save_data with (precip) for Z.
```

Note how simple this piece of code is. The list into which data will be loaded is created, two lists are created and filled to identify the fields and to control output formatting. The rest of the code is four calls to specific functions with a few display lines telling the user what is going on.

The data list 'precip', loaded from the database file with the first function call, is sent to all functions, but only two change its contents and return a revised list. 'z' is simply a placeholder in the function calls for those functions that don't return a value.

Once the data has been loaded into the 'precip' list, the user can scroll through the list six entries at a time. The user is then presented with the 'get_new' function to enter new data, after which the data in the list is saved to the database file and the program ends. Each successive run of the program will display an ever-growing list of data, unless the user elects to start with a fresh file at the beginning prompt.

Output Formatting:

The two lists, fields and formats, are key to creating functions that can be copied intact from one program to another (Chapter 11). By creating and filling these lists in the main program, functions can access data that is unique for each program through generic parameters. So, the same 'show_all' function to display data can be used for a membership database, an inventory program, or a personal stock portfolio.

Starting with the fields list, every field should have a name that appears as a column header for the data that appears in each column. With some forethought, you can jigger the name so that it also can be used as a prompt in add_new and edit routines, making these routines more-or-less generic as well.

Columns need format control to keep data aligned and reduce ragged edges. The formats list contains the codes for each field to instruct the display function how to format the data being displayed. An '18C', for example, signifies an 18-character field with the data centered.

Both the fields and formats lists are used by the various functions, but the functions use the len(fields) function in the loops, allowing them to accommodate any database program you copy them into. A membership database may have only eight fields; and inventory program might have twenty. No matter. The repeat loop will cycle only eight times in the first example, and twenty times in the second.

Slicing and Dicing Strings

Regarding formatting output, you can create left-, right- and center-justified strings within a field of a given width using concatenation. With database output, these techniques are of paramount importance. The following paragraphs describe how this is done.

To left justify, pad blanks onto the end of the string and slice from the beginning for the desired width. Note the use of a colon within the slice operation.

```
Assign 20 to width.
Assign name+" "*50 to adj_name.
Display adj_name[0:width]
```

To right justify, pad blanks in front of the string and count backward from the end the desired width, slicing from there to the end. If either beginning or ending slice designations are missing, slicing assumes first and last elements in the string.

```
Assign 20 to width.
Assign " "*50+ name to adj_name.
Display adj_name[-width:].
```

Center justification requires padding both front and back. Then find the center and count backward half the desired width to start the slice, and from center forward half the width to end the slice.

```
Assign 20 to width.
Assign " "*50+ name + " "*50 to adj_name.
Assign int(len(adj_name)/2) to midpt.
Dislay adj_name[midpt-int(width/2):midpt+int(width/2)].
```

For this program, with only three fields, the fields and formats lists in the main program look like this:

```
Create list fields.
Create list formats.
Add "Date (dd/mm/yy)","Temp.(C)","Precip.(cm)" to list fields.
Add "18C","10C","12C" to list formats.
```

The first list will be used for the header row and for the prompts for data entry for each of the fields in the record. The second list combines field width and justification flags for each field. We can slice this formatting data into integers for field width and 'L', 'C', or 'R' for justification flags. (See below.) This gives us exquisite output formatting control.

The file I/O Operations:

```
Comment: Demo12.1 List of Records, Daily Precip.

 [Function save_data using (listname):
     Create file precip.csv.
     Copy database from listname to precip.csv.
     Display "Data is now saved.".
     Return "".
     End of function block.]


[Function get_data using (listname):
    Assign "X" to newfile.
    [Repeat block while newfile == "X" with idx:
        Display "Start a fresh file? (Y/N)".
        Get string for newfile.
        Assign newfile.upper() to newfile.
        [If (newfile == "Y") then:
            Create file precip.csv.
            End of if block.]
        [If newfile == "N" then:
            Display "Retrieving data from file.".
            Copy database from precip.csv to listname.
            End of if block.]
        [If newfile != "Y" and newfile != "N" then:
            Assign "X" to newfile.
            End of if block.]
        End of repeat block.]
    Return listname.
    End of function block.]
```

With KwicKode, filenames must be presented with their
.csv or .txt suffix. So, using generic parameter names for file
names won't work. In these two functions, there are three
places where a filename appears, and it is the specific
filename required for this particular program. With this
exception, these two functions are otherwise identical to their

counterparts in the membership database program, Demo12.2. You can use them over and over again.

At the start, the user may elect to erase the file and start over. The function then either creates a new .csv file or retrieves the old data, depending on the user's decision. If a new file is desired, but old data is to be retained, then the three filenames in these two functions need to be changed to the name of the new file before the program is run.

Displaying the Records:

Functions show_data and show_one display the database list of records. Show_data controls the looping process and calls show_one for each record to be displayed. Additionally, show_one is the perfect function for the edit, delete, and search functions in program 12.2. So, it makes sense to create a generic function to handle all these requirements.

As for show_all, rather than scroll through the entire list to the end, only ten records are shown at a time. (This value can be changed in the function call's argument list in the Main Program, so using 'group' to represent this value makes that aspect generic.) At each pause, the user may elect to scroll forward to the next ten records, scroll back, or quit the display process entirely by entering 'M' for menu.

To make this happen, the function makes use of nested loops. The outer loop cycles through the entire dataset using 'k' for a counter and len(listname) to determine when all the records have been displayed. But the inner loop runs just

'group' cycles at a time, after which the short menu described
above is displayed.

After 'group' (i.e. ten, here) items have been displayed,
the outer loop counter is behind by that many items. So
before looping back, 'k' must be adjusted upward to account
for the ten items just displayed, with Assign k+j-1 to k. (The
'minus one' is necessary because at the end of j's loop, j was
automatically incremented.)

```
[Function show_data using (listname,group):
  Assign "X" to choice.
  [Repeat block while (k<len(listname) and choice!="M") with k:
    [Repeat block while (j<group and (k+j)<len(listname)) with j:
      Call function show_one with (listname[k+j],j) for z.
      End of repeat block.]
    Assign "<Enter> for next; <B> for back; <M> for menu. " to menu.
    Display menu.
    Get string for choice.
    Assign choice.upper() to choice.
    [If choice=="" and k+j-1 < len(listname)then:
       Assign k+j-1 to k.
       End of if block.]
    [Else:
      [If (choice=="B") then:
         Assign (j+k)-2*group to k.
         [If k < 0 then:
            Assign -1 to k.
            End of if block.]
         End of if block.]
      [If (choice not in "BM") then:
         Display "Invalid entry. Try again.".
         End of if block.]
      End of else block.]
  End of repeat block.]
  Return "".
End of function block.]
```

This function controls the display process but does not perform the output of either the header line or the data. For that, the function show_one is called by the inner loop with the loop counter 'j'. If this counter is zero, indicating the first of the ten records, the function show-one displays the header row. Otherwise, it just displays a row of data.

After the desired number of data rows is displayed, a brief menu prompt appears allowing the user to see the next group of data, scroll back to a previous screen, or exit the data display completely. Note that for the forward and backward scroll routines, the value for 'k', the main loop counter, must be adjusted with 'j' to account for the inner loop cycles. **This is a unique feature of KwicKode in that loop counters are not sequestered within the loop controls but are available to be adjusted as desired by the programmer.**

Since the loop counters are used here for list indexing, checks must be made that their values are always valid (not negative or not exceeding the size of the list) for the list they refer to. Otherwise, the program will crash with an 'Index out of Range' error.

The show_one function retrieves just one record from the list of data along with a flag to indicate whether to output a header row or not (see above.) For the header row, each of the field names in the fields list filled by the main program is displayed centered in the field using the widths specified in the formats list.

Similarly, the data in the specific record sent to show_one is broken out, item by item, and displayed justified as specified in a field of the specified width. The same technique used in Tic-Tac-Toe for Two to parse the format code into row and column is used here.

Because of the effort taken to generalize these two functions, Demo12.2, which follows, uses them exactly as they appear here. You can simply copy and paste them into that program when you are ready to write your code for it.

```
[Function show_one using (record,hdrflag):
  Assign "" to hdr.
  [If hdrflag == 0 then:
    [Repeat block while k<len(fields) with k:
        Assign int(formats[k][0:-1]) to width.
        Assign " "*50+fields[k]+" "*50 to a.
        Assign int(len(a)/2) to midpt.
        Assign a[midpt-int(width/2):midpt+int(width/2)] to a.
        Assign hdr + a to hdr.
        End of repeat block.]
    Display "*"*15*len(fields).
    Display hdr.
    Display "="*15*len(fields).
    End of if block.]
  Assign "" to row.
  [Repeat block while k<len(fields) with k:
      Assign int(formats[k][0:-1]) to width.
      Assign formats[k][-1] to justn.
      [If justn == "L" then:
          Assign record[k]+" "*50 to b.
          Assign row + b[0:width] to row.
          End of if block.]
      [If justn == "R" then:
          Assign " "*50+record[k] to b.
          Assign row + b[-width:] to row.
          End of if block.]
      [If justn == "C" then:
          Assign " "*50+record[k]+" "*50 to b.
          Assign int(len(b)/2) to midpt.
          Assign b[midpt-int(width/2):midpt+int(width/2)] to b.
          Assign row + b to row.
```

```
            End of if block.]
        End of repeat block.]
    Display row.
    Display "-"*15*len(fields).
   Return "".
   End of function block.]
```

Adding Fresh Data:

```
[Function get_new using (listname):
  Assign "" to entry.
  [Repeat block while entry not in "Qq" with k:
    Create list new_data.
    [Repeat block while j<len(fields) with j:
        Display "Enter "+fields[j]+" (or Q to quit.) ".
        Get string for entry.
        [If entry not in "Qq" then:
           Add entry to list new_data.
           End of if block.]
        [Else:
           Assign len(fields) to j.
           End of else block.]
        End of repeat block.]
    [If entry not in "Qq" then:
       Add new_data to list listname.
       End of if block.]
    End of repeat block.]
  Return listname.
  End of function block.]
```

The get_new function is used for data entry. Several entries may be made at once. Since this is a database we are working with, all of the data for a single record must be included in its own list. Thus the list 'new_data' is refreshed at the start of each cycle. The rest of the function consists of a series of prompts (from the fields list) and keyboard entry for each of the fields in the record. Again, by having these defined in a list, a loop handles this process without having to have separate lines of code for each field. At the end of the cycle, the 'new_data' list is added to the database list.

With slight modification, this program could be used as a bank checkbook register with an additional column for description, and the last column for the running balance which would be automatically calculated from the previous balance and the credit or debit entered into the next-to-last column. Now that you know how the fields and formats lists work, the creation of additional columns for more data should be a 'walk in the park.'

A Dynamic Database –
The Club Membership Program

You should now have a clear picture about setting up a membership database program or an inventory program patterned on the functions used in Demo12.1. Of course, these applications need additional functions that search for a specific record and that allow a particular record to be edited or deleted. A sorting function might also be helpful (Chapter 13). Since the data within this type of database can be changed over time, it is said to be a **dynamic database**.

Editing capabilities are required for when a member changes their phone number or moves to a new address or gets married. Or when an item in inventory has a price change or supplier change. A menu function like the one described in

Chapter 11 that allows the user to select from the variety of actions just described will also be needed.

Demo12.2 provides a good start toward meeting these requirements. Variations on the functions in Demo12.1 are present, as well as additional functions to address the activities just described. The option to display records has been enhanced with a user-controlled mechanism for viewing just six records at a time and for scrolling backward as well as forward, just as in Demo12.1

Python includes a wonderful list sorting method, '.sort()' Simply attach the 'dot-sort' method to your function name and the list contents get sorted without further ado. This works if the sorting is to be done with the first item in the record. Chapter 13 concentrates on methods to sort on other fields.

Don't be daunted at the length of Demo12.2. It covers a lot of bases. But you have learned all of the KwicKode commands it uses, so you should be able to read and understand everything this program code has to offer. Run the program, add some data, and see how it responds to the coded commands for each of the functions.

Main Program:

With this program, an extensive menu of options is provided to the user. Each possible selection must be handled with its own conditional test followed by either a function call or a few lines of code to deal with the selection. For this program, that code is included in the main program, right after the function call to the menu.

Demo12.2's Main Program differs from the previous static database program in that a larger menu is involved, so that the conditional branching for the program based on menu selection is done from within the Main Program. Other than that, you can readily see the similarities.

As with Demo12.1, the field titles and their formats are enumerated in two lists at the start of the program. Since the elements in these lists are constants, the lists are never changed during the program and thus do not have to be included in either argument lists or parameter lists when functions are called and executed.

After calling get_list, which is identical to Demo12.1 except for the two occurrences of the filename, a loop is set up to cycle through the program functions until the user selects the 'Q. Quit' menu option.

Within the loop, the Main Menu is called first to obtain the user's selection, which is returned and used in eight conditional statements, one for each possible menu choice. Choosing 'Q' sets the quit flag to 'Y' and ends the loop and the program. Since the sort operation in Demo12.2 requires only a single line using Python's '.sort()' method, that operation is taken care of without a function call. All the remaining choice possibilities involve functon calls.

The show_data, show_one, and add_new functions are identical to their counterparts in Demo12.1, being generalized sufficiently to be used here.

```
Comment: "*********************************".
Comment: "   Main Program Begins Here.
Create list fields.
Create list formats.
Create list members.
Add "Name:","Email:","Phone:" to list fields.
Add "Yrs:","Addr1:","Addr2:" to list fields.
Add "15L","20L","15C","6C","25L","25L" to list formats.
Call function get_data with (members) for members.
Assign "Member Database" to mdb.
Assign "Add","Edit", "Remove","Find" to list opts.
Add "Display","Sort","Copy data to archives" to list opts.
Add "Quit program" to list opts.
Assign "AERFDSCQ" to codes.
Assign "N" to quit.
[Repeat block while quit == "N" with m:
   Call function db_menu with (mdb,opts,codes) for seln.
   [If seln == "A" then:
     Call function get_new with (members) for members.
     End of if block.]
   [If seln == "E" then:
      Call function edit with (members) for members.
     End of if block.]
   [If seln == "R" then:
      Call function delete with (members) for members.
     End of if block.]
   [If seln == "F" then:
      Call function search with (members, "") for idx.
     End of if block.]
   [If seln == "D" then:
      Call function show_data with (members,6) for Z.
     End of if block.]
   [If seln == "S" then:
      Assign members.sort() to Z.
      Display "Your data has been sorted.".
     End of if block.]
   [If seln == "C" then:
      Create file members.csv.
      Call function save_data with (members) for Z.
     End of if block.]
   [If seln == "Q" then:
```

```
        Assign "Y" to quit.
        End of if block.]
  End of repeat block.]
```

The File I/O Operations:

As mentioned in the File I/O section for the previous
program, the same two functions appear here, identical
except for the three references to the specific data file
containing this program's data. Their code is repeated here.

```
Comment: Demo12.2 Membership Database.
Comment: by Bishop, 1/29/25.
[Function get_data using (listname):
   Assign "X" to newfile.
   [Repeat block while newfile == "X" with idx:
      Display "Start a fresh file? (Y/N)".
      Get string for newfile.
      Assign newfile.upper() to newfile.
      [If (newfile == "Y") then:
         Create file members.csv.
         End of if block.]
      [If newfile == "N" then:
         Display "Retrieving data from file.".
         Copy database from members.csv to listname.
         End of if block.]
      [If newfile != "Y" and newfile != "N" then:
         Assign "X" to newfile.
         End of if block.]
      End of repeat block.]
   Return listname.
   End of function block.]

[Function save_data using (listname):
   Create file precip.csv.
   Copy database from listname to members.csv.
   Display "Data is now saved.".
   Return "".
   End of function block.]
```

A Generalized Menu Routine:

As described in Chapter 11, a generalized menu function that is restricted to presenting a menu, obtaining a single-character response from the user, and validating that response, can be used in many different programs. The only changes in the main_menu function in this program from Chapter 11's menu code is that in this program, the database is automatically loaded at the beginning. So the 'G' option in both conditional statements, and the 'G-Get database' prompt have been removed.

```
Comment: Get users choice from menu of options.
[Function db_menu using (db_name, options, choices):
    Display "Database "+db_name+" Main Menu: ".
    Assign "X" to choice.
    [Repeat block while choice not in choices with z:
        [Repeat block while cnt < len(choices) with cnt:
            Display choices[cnt]+ " - "+options[cnt].
            End of repeat block.]
        Display "Enter your selection... ".
        Get string for choice.
        Assign choice.upper() to choice.
        [If choice not in choices then:
            Display "Not a valid choice. Try again.".
            End of if block.]
        End of repeat block.]
    Return choice.
    End of function block.]
```

The Search Function:

Next comes the search function.

```
Comment: Search for a specific record by name.
[Function search using (listname, name):
   [If name == "" then:
      Display "Enter data to search for. ".
      Get string for name.
      End of if block.]
   Assign -1 to idx.
   [Repeat block while k<len(listname) with k:
      [If listname[k][0] == name then:
         Assign k to idx.
         Call function show_one with (listname[idx], 0)
               for Z.
         Display "Is this the record you wanted? (Y/N): ".
         Get string for ans.
         Assign ans.upper() to ans.
         [If ans == "Y" then:
            Assign len(listname) to k.
            End of if block.]
         [Else:
            Assign -1 to idx.
            End of else block.]
         End of if block.]
      End of repeat block.]
   [If idx != -1 then:
      Call function show_one with (listname[idx], 0) for Z.
      End of if block.]
   [Else:
      Display "No match was found. Try again.".
      End of else block.]
   Return idx.
End of function block.]
```

One of the menu options is 'S-Search' for when the user wants to pull a specific record from the database to view. But this function must also be used by the 'E. Edit' and 'D.

Delete' options to find the record to be edited or deleted. So this function is generalized to be used in any database search whatsoever. The function does have one shortcoming, in that the search is limited to the first field in the record database.

A successful search will result in a call to show_one to display a single record, and the value returned is that record's index number. If -1 is returned, that tells the calling routine that no record was found. However, if a match is found, the user is shown the record and asked if it is the one desired. If not, the search will continue to the next match and repeat the process. So multiple records having the same value in the first field can be located.

Displaying Records:

The show_data function and the show_one function, which is called by the former to actually display a record, are identical to those used in Demo12.1. The advantage of generalizing functions is clearly demonstrated here.

```
[Function show_data using (listname,group):
  Assign "X" to choice.
  [Repeat block while (k<len(listname) and choice!="M") with k:
    [Repeat block while j<group and k+j<len(listname) with j:
      Call function show_one with (listname[k+j],j) for z.
      End of repeat block.]
    Assign "<Enter> for next; <B> for back; <M> for menu. " to menu.
    Display menu.
    Get string for choice.
    Assign choice.upper() to choice.
    [If choice=="" and k+j-1 < len(listname) then:
      Assign k+j-1 to k.
      End of if block.]
    [Else:
      [If (choice=="B") then:
        Assign (j+k)-2*group-2 to k.
        [If k < 0 then:
          Assign -1 to k.
          End of if block.]
        End of if block.]
      [If (choice not in "BM") then:
        Display "Invalid entry. Try again.".
        End of if block.]
      End of else block.]
  End of repeat block.]
  Return "".
End of function block.]
```

```
[Function show_one using (record,hdrflag):
  Assign "" to hdr.
  [If hdrflag == 0 then:
     [Repeat block while k<len(fields) with k:
        Assign int(formats[k][0:-1]) to width.
        Assign " "*50+fields[k]+" "*50 to a.
        Assign int(len(a)/2) to midpt.
        Assign a[midpt-int(width/2):midpt+int(width/2)] to a.
        Assign hdr + a to hdr.
        End of repeat block.]
     Display "*"*15*len(fields).
     Display hdr.
     Display "="*15*len(fields).
     End of if block.]
  Assign "" to row.
  [Repeat block while k<len(fields) with k:
     Assign int(formats[k][0:-1]) to width.
     Assign formats[k][-1] to justn.
     [If justn == "L" then:
        Assign record[k]+" "*50 to b.
        Assign row + b[0:width] to row.
        End of if block.]
     [If justn == "R" then:
        Assign " "*50+record[k] to b.
        Assign row + b[-width:] to row.
        End of if block.]
     [If justn == "C" then:
        Assign " "*50+record[k]+" "*50 to b.
        Assign int(len(b)/2) to midpt.
        Assign b[midpt-int(width/2):midpt+int(width/2)] to b.
        Assign row + b to row.
        End of if block.]
     End of repeat block.]
  Display row.
  Display "-"*15*len(fields).
  Return "".
  End of function block.]
```

Add, Edit, and Delete Records

Now we are down to the 'A-Add', 'E-Edit', and 'D-Delete' functions. These bear a similarity in that they operate on a single record. With 'add', blank data entry fields must be filled in. With 'edit', the fields show the current data, and by not changing data in a field, the old data is preserved.

Function get_new is the same generalized function you saw in Demo12.1 and as such, can be used in many other programs. Note again that by defining a list in the Main Program to contain the field names, and then using elements from that list here for the prompts, this function is totally generalized for any program, anytime.

```
[Function get_new using (listname):
  Assign "" to entry.
  [Repeat block while entry != "0" with k:
    Create list new_data.
    [Repeat block while j<len(fields) with j:
      Display "Enter "+fields[j]+" (or 0 to quit.) ".
      Get string for entry.
      [If entry != "0" then:
        Add entry to list new_data.
        End of if block.]
      [Else:
        Assign len(fields) to j.
        End of else block.]
      End of repeat block.]
    [If entry != "0" then:
      Add new_data to list listname.
      End of if block.]
    End of repeat block.]
  Return listname.
  End of function block.]
```

The edit function works the same way, and it too is totally generalized, so long as no entry validation checks are required. Also, since the fields list is defined in the Main Program and isn't changed in any of these functions, it doesn't even need to be added to the functions' parameter lists.

```
[Function edit using (listname):
  Display "Enter search data for record that needs
editing.".
  Get string for item.
  Call function search with (listname,item) for idx.
  Comment: Search returns -1 if search failed.
  [If idx != -1 then:
    Display "Enter new data or press <Enter> to skip.".
    [Repeat block while k<len(listname[idx]) with k:
      Display fields[k]+ ": "+listname[idx][k].
      Get string for chg.
      [If chg != "" then:
        Assign chg to listname[idx][k].
        End of if block.]
      End of repeat block.]
    Call function show_one with (listname[idx],0) for z.
    End of if block.]
  Return listname.
  End of function block.]
```

Finally, the delete function. This function, like the edit function, calls for a specific record. Once the record is displayed, the user is given a chance to back off by being specifically asked if this is the record to be deleted. If the user consents, the record is deleted and control is returned to the main program. Otherwise, the database is left unchanged.

```
Comment: Find and delete a specific record.
[Function delete using (listname):
  Display "Enter search data for record to be deleted. ".
  Get string for item.
  Call function search with (listname, item) for idx.
  [If idx != -1 then:
    Comment: Double check before deleting.
    Display "Enter 'YES' to delete record.".
    Get string for del_record.
    Assign del_record.upper() to del_record.
    [If del_record == "YES" then:
      Display listname[idx][0],"has been removed.".
      Remove listname[idx] from list listname.
      End of if block.]
    End of if block.]
  Return listname.
  End of function block.]
```

In this lesson you have learned how to create both static and dynamic databases, entering and storing data for future use, and how to search, edit, and delete records from these files. You have learned the advantages of generalizing your functions to make them available for future programs and to avoid reinventing the wheel.

```
Create file filename.
Copy database listname to filename.
Copy database filename to listname.
```

In addition, you have learned several terms associated with databases.

static database   **dynamic database**
record   **generalizing functions**

Chapter 13
Sorting Records

The Club Membership program in the previous section allowed sorting to occur for just the first field in the record. But there are many occasions where you may wish to temporarily sort the records on one of the other fields. This chapter shows two ways to accomplish this.

The first approach uses only KwicKode commands and doesn't even use the Python '.sort( )' method found in Demo12.2. It takes advantage of two nested loops. The idea is to compare the first record (outer loop) with each of the records below it (inner loop). When one of the lower record's fields evaluates to less than the current outer loop record, a swap is made, thus placing the lower valued record on top.

When this first cycling through the inner loop is finished, the lowest valued record has been weeded from its original location and placed at the top. Now the outer loop cycles to record number two, and the same process takes place for it. By the time the outer loop completes its cycling, all the records have been sorted.

Demo13.1 is a short program that demonstrates how this works. The sort_data function in this program is generalized and can be adopted for any database program where lists need to be sorted by various fields.

```
Comment: Demo13.1 Sorting a list on any field.

Comment: idx is the index number of the desired field.
[Function sort_data using (testlist, idx):
    [Repeat block while k < (len(testlist)-1) with k:
        [Repeat block while j < len(testlist) with j:
            [If not (j  > k) then:
                Assign k+1 to j.
                End of if block.]
            [If testlist[j][idx] < testlist[k][idx] then:
                Assign testlist[k] to holder.
                Assign testlist[j] to testlist[k].
                Assign holder to testlist[j].
                End of if block.]
            End of repeat block.]
        End of repeat block.]
    Return testlist.
    End of function block.]

[Function get_data using (testsort):
    Assign "Y" to more.
    [Repeat block while more == "Y" with k:
        Create list record.
        Display "Enter a name.".
        Get string for name.
        Add name to list record.
        Display "Enter a 2-digit age.".
        Get string for age.
        Add age to list record.
        Display "Enter a zip code.".
        Get string for zip.
        Add zip to list record.
        Add record to list testsort.
        Display "More? (Y/N)".
        Get string for more.
        Assign more.upper() to more.
        End of repeat block.]
    Display testsort as list.
    Return testsort.
    End of function block.]
```

```
Comment: Main Program.
Create list testsort.
Call function get_data with (testsort) for testsort.
Display "Sorting by age.".
Call function sort_data with (testsort, 1) for testsort.
Display testsort as list.
Display "Sorting by zip code.".
Call function sort_data with (testsort, 2) for testsort.
Display testsort as list.
Display "Sorting by name.".
Call function sort_data with (testsort, 0) for testsort.
Display testsort as list.
```

A second approach to sorting records on any field uses Python's built in '.sort( )' method, which operates on the first field, along with a bit of computer trickery to get the data in the desired field to temporarily appear first.

Three Python methods must be used to create this magic. If the sort field is the first field, then a single '.sort( )' command is all that is needed. Otherwise, we need to loop through all the records and, if the sort field is not the last field, we can add a copy of the data in the sort field to the end of the record. Then we perform a '.reverse( )' method to get all the fields in the record presented in reverse order. Voila! The desired field's data is in First Place. The loop continues to the last record. All of the records are ready now for the '.sort( )' method.

The '.sort( )' method performs the desired sort. Now another loop must be used to turn each record around so the fields are in their expected order with another '.reverse( )' method, and, if it was necessary to add a field, the '.pop( )'

method is used to get rid of that extra field. The database is now sorted by the selected field.

Fortunately, to return to the original sort order, a single '.sort( )' is all that is needed, sorting the database on the standard first field. (Assuming the database was in order when we started.)

The function below handles this operation, and includes the menu asking the user which field should be used for the sort. This function can be added as-is to the Membership Program, Demo12.2. The only line in the Main Program that needs to be replaced is the

```
Assign members.sort() to Z.
```

line in the "S" selection conditional block. Replace it with the function call:

```
Call function sort_data with (members,fields) for Z.
```

```
Comment: Sort data on a selected field.
[Function sort_data using (listname,fields):
    Assign "False" to entry.
    [Repeat block while entry == "False" with z:
        [Repeat block while k<len(fields) with k:
            Display k, ": ",fields[k].
            End of repeat block.]
        Display "Enter index # for field to be sorted. ".
        Get string for idx.
        Assign int(idx) to idx.
        [If idx >= 0 and idx < len(fields) then:
            Assign "True" to entry.
            End of if block.]
        End of repeat block.]
    [If idx == 0 then:
```

```
      Assign listname.sort() to z.
      End of if block.]
 [Else:
    [If idx == len(fields)-1 then:
       [Repeat block while k < len(listname) with k:
          Assign listname[k].reverse() to z.
          End of repeat block.]
       Assign listname.sort() to z.
       [Repeat block while k < len(listname) with k:
          Assign listname[k].reverse() to z.
          End of repeat block.]
       End of if block.]
    [Else:
       [Repeat block while k < len(listname) with k:
          Add listname[k][idx] to list listname[k].
          Assign listname[k].reverse() to z.
          End of repeat block.]
       Assign listname.sort() to z.
       [Repeat block while k < len(listname) with k:
          Assign listname[k].reverse() to z.
          Assign listname[k].pop() to z.
          End of repeat block.]
       End of else block.]
    End of else block.]
 Return ().
 End of function block.]
```

Since this function is totally generalized due to the fields list, it could easily be inserted into the Daily Precipitation database program with no modifications, allowing that database to be sorted by temperature or by precipitation. The only changes needed to the main program would be an options menu for the user to select 'SORT' and a function call as described above.

These sort functions are the only functions in this manual that are not straightforward applications of coding commands. You likely would not have come up with a method for sorting by different fields at this point in your coding experience. That is to be expected. As with any professional skill, these insights come only through practice and experience. But as you tackle progressively more challenging problems, you will continually add to your knowledge and insight.

In the short time you have been studying KwicKode, you have learned the fundamentals of computer programming and coding. With nothing more than these KwicKode commands, you can write many relatively sophisticated programs. You are also well positioned to jump into more robust languages, such as Python, Java, and C++. With your understanding of KwicKode, you will be surprised at how fast you will progress in these other languages should you decide to go in that direction.

In this lesson you have learned how to sort records in a database on any of the fields using two different techniques, the first using 'raw' KwicKode commands and the second using built-in Python functions embedded in KwicKode Assignment statements. Both sorting functions are generalized, making them available for use in any program that requires sorting data in a list. to make them available for future programs and to avoid reinventing the wheel.

The Python methods used in this chapter for sorting lists on any field take no parameters. They are:

.sort( )   .reverse( )   .pop( )

Chapter 14
Springboard to Python

Depending on your goals and aspirations, you may now have everything you need in the way of computer coding knowledge. You are now familiar with all the major operations required to make a computer do your bidding. KwicKode may be sufficient for your personal coding needs. But if you devoted these past few days with an eye to jumping into Python, this chapter will help you make that transition.

All the KwicKode programs you have written are saved to your computer as text files. Furthermore, all the corresponding Python files the compiler created from them are also saved on your computer. Both files have the same name, one with a '.txt' suffix, the other with a '.py' suffix. You can load them both in side-by-side windows using the Python IDLE editor. With both files on your screen, you can compare the Python code with the KwicKode code. This can be an invaluable tool for getting started with Python. Start with Demo1.1 and work forward from there. You will be surprised at how quickly you catch on to Python syntax.

That said, the rest of this chapter is devoted to elaborating on the similarities and differences between KwicKode and Python to help codify the Python programming syntax into your mind. In fact, after an hour or two, you will be able to write Python programs into the IDLE editor and run them. It may seem as though you have been studying Python all along. You are more than ready to tackle more detailed Python manuals or to begin Python classes. Your newly developed knowledge is the foundation for future success in computer coding. Good luck!!

General Observations

1. **No caps. No periods. No required Comments.**
   Python does not use capital letters or periods to begin and end program lines. Until you get to the subject of 'classes', all lettering is lower case. (Although, some programmers prefer 'camel code' for multi-word variable names, such as myFriend, as an alternative to using underscores.) Python does not require programs to begin with a comment statement. (Still good coding practice, though.) And speaking of comments, Python's symbol for starting a comment line is the hash mark, '#':

```
# This Python comment line is totally ignored
```

2. **Program blocks: Indentation is required, but no square brackets and no 'End of block…' terminator command.**
   Python does not use square brackets to enclose blocks of code, nor does it use a block-ending statement like 'End of if block.]' Blocks of code are only identified by the **first line ending in a colon** and following lines having **required** indentation. The end of indentation signifies the end of the block.

3. Variable names and function names in Python follow the same rules you have learned for KwicKode.

4. List elements are indexed the same way in both Python and KwicKode and both languages identify list elements with index numbers in square brackets. Index numbering begins at zero. Index slicing also works the same in both languages.

5. Python's 'print(...)' function serves the same role as KwicKode's 'Display...' command, with parentheses required.

```
print(my_friend, " is ",friends_age, " today.")
```

Everything you have been placing after the word 'Display' can be placed inside the print function's parentheses. But Python has a wealth of additional features to control output. These features can also be used in KwicKode, but have been omitted from this manual to keep things as simple as possible.

6. Assignment statements use a single '=' symbol (NOT to be read as 'equals'; rather, read it as 'is assigned'.)

```
member_name = "Betsy"
        instead of:
Assign "Betsy" to member_name.

my_age = 21
        instead of:
Assign 21 to my_age.
```

So, the value to be assigned comes at the end of the statement, and the variable name at the start, exactly the reverse of the order used by KwicKode. Instead of:

7. Python uses the input(...) function for keyboard input. The syntax is:

    ```
    age = input("How old are you? ")
    ```

    Note that the single string prompt in Python is part of the input command, whereas KwicKode required a separate 'Display...' command. Also note that the variable receiving the string input from the keyboard appears before the assignment '=' symbol.

8. Python's conditional 'if...:' and 'else:' commands look much like KwicKode's if you remove the word 'then'. They still require the colon, being the first statement in a coding block. Indentation is required in Python.

    ```
    if entry == "Q":
        Code block if condition is true
    else:
        Code block if condition is false
    ```

    (No brackets, and no 'End of ... block.]' termination lines.)

9. Conditional expressions are written exactly the same in both KwicKode and in Python. Don't forget to double the '==' symbol for 'equals'.

10. Python has an additional command, 'elif (...):' , that works like an 'else:' followed by another 'if...:' statement. This command keeps successive conditional statements in line, avoiding having indentations running off the page! It is very useful for menus and other multiple-choice option

considerations. It is also more efficient than successive multiple 'if...' commands.

```
if choice == "A":
        code block
elif choice == "B":
        code block
elif choice == "C":
        code block
else:
        code block
```

11. Conditional expressions and mathematical expressions work the same way in both languages. However, to use advanced math functions (trig functions, for example), random functions, or .csv file functions, you must import the appropriate modules at the very top of your program, such as:

```
import csv
import math
from random import choice
```

The first two import the whole module. (A module is a collection of functions.) The third imports only the selected function from the specified module. If you use a function from the first case, you must specify the module as well, using 'dot notation', as in :

```
x = math.cos(0.9876)
```

12. The first line in a function block in Python begins with 'def' followed by the function name, the function's

parameter list in parentheses, and a colon. The words 'function' and 'using' do not appear.

```
def main_menu (cntr, sum):
```

User defined functions must appear before the main program sequence, just as in KwicKode. All lines other than the first must be indented.

13. The last line in a Python function block, indented along with the other lines, is the 'return ...' command, with the value to be returned represented by the ellipsis. This is just like the KwicKode 'Return...' command without the ending period.

14. Function calls in Python are written as assignment statements (see above), where the value being returned by the function is assigned to the variable to the left of the assignment '=' symbol.

```
new_yr = add1(yr)
```

If no values are being returned, just the mention of the function name calls the function. No dummy variables are needed.

```
show_calendar(May, 2024)
```

15. Python has a variety of additional options for handling arguments and parameters that provide greater flexibility for the coder's tool box. Be sure to check them out when you are ready.

16. The 'while' loop in Python is similar to its KwicKode counterpart, without the words '[Repeat block'. It controls a block of code identified only by indentation. KwicKode offers a built-in loop counter with this type of loop, but Python does not. If you need a counter such as idx with a 'while...' loop, initialize it before the loop, and increment it at the end of the loop, as shown below.

```
idx = 0
while choice != "Q":
      code block
      idx = idx + 1
program continues here.
```

Incidentally to increment or decrease a variable by a certain value, Python offers a useful shortcut:

```
idx += 1
```

17. The iterative loop in Python has a totally different look from KwicKode's single loop command. It still controls a block, with the colon and indentation being the only (and required) identifiers for block operation.

```
for  k in range(0,10):
      code block
program continues here.
```

One thing to note about this syntax is that the loop counter 'k' can be accessed within the loop for list indexing, displaying, etc., but it cannot be altered by assigning it a different value. Also, once the loop has ended, Python forgets it ever existed. Often, coders choose a single letter like i, j, or k for their loop counters and use them over and over again within the same program.

Another point is how the 'range(…)' function works. The first number in parentheses is the starting value for the counter, while the second is **one higher than the last value** for the counter. So, for 'range(0,10)', the counter takes on ten values from zero to nine. This works perfectly for list indexing, where a list with ten elements is indexed from zero to nine, and the length function, len(…), returns 10. So:

```
for m in range(0, len(my_list)):
    print(m+1, ":    ", my_list[m] )
```

18. Regarding indexed lists in Python, the good news is that Python and KwicKode share the same syntax. To access an element in a list, follow the list name with the index number of the element enclosed in square brackets.

19. Creating a list in Python is done with a simple assignment statement using an empty set of brackets, or a list of specifically defined elements within brackets.

```
members = []
my_pets = ["Cleo", "Hermy", "Spot"]
```

20. Adding to and deleting from a list uses two of Python's built-in list methods. As with KwicKode, an added item is added to the end of a list, while for deletions, the first match encountered is deleted from the list. The two methods are '.append(…)' and '.remove(…)':

```
my_pets.append("Lizzy")
my_pets.remove("Cleo")
```

21. All of the list-related functions and methods you have used in KwicKode were adopted from Python, so they all work the same way in Python.These include the len(…) function and the '.index(…)' '.count(…)' '.pop( )', and '. sort( )', methods

File I/O in Python

Python file I/O is beyond the scope of this simple introduction to coding. The single KwicKode command for saving and retrieving lists to .csv and .txt files is implemented by dozens of lines of Python code. Furthermore, .txt and .csv formats are only two of several different types of file formats in common use. Each type has its own peculiar set of commands and options.

Since file I/O can be complicated, it usually isn't covered until the end of a semester-long class. You will have learned a lot more about Python and coding by then. The mysteries and nuances of file I/O will be revealed when it is time. In the meantime, feel free to simply copy the Python code produced by KwicKode's single 'Copy database…' command and make whatever modifications you need to affix that code to your Python programs.

Appendix A —
KwicKode Commands

Command	Description
Comment: …. .	The ellipsis may contain anything. KwicKode ignores comment lines. However, the first line of every program MUST be a comment line. Colons and ending period are required.
Display …. Display…as list.	Contents of *ellipsis* are displayed in the shell window. If 'as list' is used, the objects are displayed in a vertical list. If the object is a single string, the letters are displayed vertically.
Assign…to *var1*. Assign…to list *var1*.	The ellipsis represents a numeric or string constant, an expression, or a variable name whose contents are assigned to *var1*. If *var1* is a list, it must be preceded by the word 'list', and multiple objects, separated by commas, may fill in for the ellipsis. The list is automatically created if nonexistent.
Get string for *var1*.	Keyboard input is assigned to *var1*. 'string' is a reminder that all input is of string type. This command MUST be preceded by a 'Display…' prompt command containing a single string.

Command	Description
[If *cond.* then:	First line in a conditional block. The commands within the block are executed only if the conditional expression is TRUE. Bracket and colon are required.
[Else:	Beginning of an optional conditional block. If the '[Else:' command is used, it MUST follow an '[If...' block. The commands within the block are executed only when the condition in the '[If...' block is FALSE.
End of ... block.]	Required ending statement for blocks. The ellipsis is 'if', 'else', 'repeat', or 'function'. Right bracket is required.
[Function *name* using (*var_list*):	First line in a function block definition. *name* is the function's name. *var_list* is a comma separated list of 0 or more variables that receive values passed to the function by the calling command. Be sure to include a space before the left parenthesis.
Return *var1*. End of function block.]	Last two lines in a function block MUST be a 'Return...' command and an 'End of function block.]'. The value in *var1* is the value passed back to the calling command, or an empty string.

Command	Description
Call function *name* with (*var. list*) for *var1*.	This command calls the named function with zero or more arguments (the *var. list*) that match 1-for-1 with the function's parameter list. *var1* receives the value passed back from the function's 'Return…' command.
[Repeat block while (*cond. expr.*) with *var1*:	Command to initiate a loop block that executes only as long as the conditional expression is True. The loop counter *var1* is automatically initialized to zero and incremented at the end of each cycle. It may be used and edited inside the loop and retains its last value for use after the block has ended. If *var1* is included in the conditional expression, an iterative (counting) loop can be set up, as in '[Repeat block while cnt < 10 with cnt:'
Create list *var1*.	Command to create an empty list named *var1*. If *var1* already exists, it is emptied.
Add … to list *var1*.	Adds one or more variables to list *var1*. Added objects are appended to the end of the list. Objects may be of any type, separated by commas. The specified list must previously exist.

Command	Description
Remove ... from list *var1*.	Removes a specified object from list *var1*. If object isn't found, a message is generated. If object appears multiple times in list, only the first is removed.
Create file *name*.	Command to create the file *name* or erase its contents if it exists already. The name must include either .txt or .csv for a suffix.
Copy data from *var1* to *var2*. Copy database from *var1* to *var2*	Command to copy the contents of *var1* into *var2*. If var1 is a list and var2 is a file, it performs a 'save' operation. If var1 is a file and var2 is a list, it performs a 'retrieve' operation. File names must have a .csv or .txt suffix. With 'save' operations, added data is appended onto end of existing data in the file. With 'retrieve' operations, the specified file is created or, if already existing, is emptied, before data is copied into it. Therefore, 'Create file...' may be needed to avoid duplication of data in the archive file. Copying data to a non-existent file automatically creates the file. Trying to read from a non-existent file results in an error message. Use the database variation for lists of lists (records)..

Appendix B —
Rules for KwicKode Syntax

1. All KwicKode programs must begin with a 'Comment:....' statement for a title, author, etc. All text after the colon is ignored except for the ending period.

2. All commands begin with a capital letter.

3. All lines must end in either a period, colon, or right bracket. The first line in a block begins with a left bracket and ends in a colon, while the last line in a block ends with a period and a right bracket, '.]', so that the entire block is enclosed in square brackets. All other lines must end in a period. If a comment is too long for one line and requires two lines, both begin with 'Comment:' and both must end with a period. This may look a bit strange if a 'Display ...' command ends with a sting containing a period, such as 'Display "Hello.".' but the period ending the command that appears outside the quotes is required.

4. Variable names must begin with a lower-case letter and be followed with lowercase letters and numbers and may include an underscored space to separate words, as in *my_name*. The same rules apply to function names.

5. The last line in a block must be 'End of ... block.]' ending with the period and right bracket. The ellipsis may be 'if', 'else', 'repeat', or 'function', specifying the block that it is associated with. The sentence has the same

indentation as the other lines within the block. It is recommended that all lines except the first in a block be indented for clarity. Doing this in KwicKode will ease the transition to Python where indentation is mandatory.

6. Strings and text must be enclosed in quotation marks except in comment lines.

7. The 'Get string...' command, like Python's 'input(...)' function, always returns a string. In KwicKode, it must be preceded by a 'Display...' command containing a single-string prompt for the input command. If a number input is desired, the returned string may be converted (type cast) to a number with either:

```
Assign (int(var1)) to var1.
   or
Assign (float(var1)) to var1.
```

8. Blocks may be nested to any level and loop blocks may be mixed with conditional blocks.

9. Function blocks must always precede the main program and may appear in any order. They may be called from the main program or from other functions. If a function calls itself, (a 'recursive' operation) the call must be part of a conditional block with a condition that eventually changes to False and terminates the process, otherwise a spiral down the bottomless rabbit-hole occurs.

10. It is good practice to organize programs so that functions act like chapters in a book. Any well-defined task within a program should be written as a separate function.

Repetitive lines of code should be put in their own function so they only appear once in the program.

11. Lists are one-dimensional arrays. However, the elements in a list may be lists themselves, thus creating two-dimensional arrays or, if extended, arrays of any dimension. Each successive subscript for multi-dimensional arrays must be contained in its own pair of brackets. Indexing always begins with zero. Thus friends_phone[18][5] would be the nineteenth record in the friends list, and within each record, the phone number is the sixth entry.

12. File names must always have either .txt or .csv suffixes attached.

13. Be sure only a single space is used to separate elements of a command line.

14. The user-defined counter in '[Repeat block while' commands is treated by KwicKode as a variable like all others. It may have its value altered within the loop by an 'Assign' command. It is also available with its last value (incremented by one) to be used even after the loop has terminated. It is automatically initialized to zero before the loop and is incremented by one just prior to the 'End of repeat block.]' command. These features are unique to KwicKode.

Appendix C —
kk_to_py_translator.py

The Python translator program, kk_to_py_translator.py that makes KwicKode possible is listed in this section. To run your KwicKode programs, you must first save them as .txt files, then run this translator program.

The first thing the translator program does is ask you to enter the name of your KwicKode file. In this case, you don't need to add the .txt suffix. The translator program first checks through your code for any obvious errors and will call your attention to these errors, usually with a line number to help you locate and correct them. (Note: The IDLE editor shows the cursor's line number in the lower right corner.)

If all goes well and it finds no errors, the translator program generates a Python program with the same name as your KwicKode program, but with the .py suffix. You may then load and run the Python program. Less obvious errors will be caught by the Python interpreter. To make corrections now, study the error message and try to identify the line in your KwicKode file that corresponds to the faulty line in the Python code. Then go back to your KwicKode program to correct the errors, and start over again. However, be sure to close the window containing the faulty Python program. Otherwise, even if you correct the error and run the translator again, when you finally run the Python program it will be the original faulty program (that hadn't been closed) that will be executed!

The kk_to_py_translator listing below is over 500 lines of code. Many lines are much too long to fit on a page, so the lines wrap into the next printed line on the page. But if you highlight the entire program (assuming you are reading a digital version of this manual), copy it to your clipboard and paste it into an empty IDLE editor window. The code will take on a regular font size and word wrap will be eliminated. The result should be a working program!

Save it using the kk_to_py_translator.py name. You will only have to enter the name once. After successfully running it the first time, it can always be found under the Files→Recent Files list and loaded into the editor with a single click.

After you have pasted the translator program into your editor and saved it, run it with Run→Run Module. If the program copied into the IDLE editor correctly, you should see the prompt asking for the name of your KwikKode file. Just press <Enter> (generating an error code, of course) and you are set up to learn and use KwicKode.

If the prompt does not appear, but red error messages appear, they are probably due to ragged indentations. Check the line numbers containing the errors and make corrections using back-space or space-bar to even things out. Then try running the program again.

'kk_to_py_translator.py' Program Listing

```
''' This program reads a KwicKode .txt file and parses and
interprets the
commands into standard Python, and saves the resulting
file as a .py file
with the same file name.'''

def get_KwicKode_filename():
    ''' Get the KwicKode file name from the user.'''
    filename = input("Enter the name of your KwicKode
.txt program...")
    if filename[-4:] != ".txt": filename = filename +
".txt"
    return filename

def load_msgs(msgs):
    msgs.append( "Error in line ")#0
    msgs.append( "Your program's first line needs to be a
'Comment:' statement,ending in a period.")#1
    msgs.append( "Statement needs a capital letter and/or
an ending period.")#2
    msgs.append( "Line needs an ending square bracket to
close a block.")#3
    msgs.append("Block initiation lines begin with a
square bracket and end with a colon.")#4
    msgs.append("Block must end with an 'End
of...block.]' command.")#5
    msgs.append("Keyboard input command 'Get...' must be
preceded with a 'Display...' prompt line.")#6
    msgs.append("Conditional statement needs a 'then:'
with a colon.")#7
    msgs.append("Repeat commands need the words 'block'
and 'with'.")#8
    msgs.append("Only a single space is allowed after the
word 'list'.")#9
    msgs.append("Line needs a beginning square bracket to
open a block. ")#10
    msgs.append("")#11
```

```
    msgs.append("Function block initiation line syntax is
'[Function ... using (param.list):' with space after
'using'.")#12
    msgs.append("Function call syntax is 'Call function
... with (arg.list) for .... with space after 'with'.")#13
    msgs.append("The 'Create...' command must be followed
by the word 'list' or 'file'.")#14
    msgs.append("The 'Copy...' command must include the
words 'from' and 'to'.")#15
    msgs.append("Your left-bracket count does not match
your right-bracket count.")#16
    msgs.append("Check your code. You are missing at
least one left or right square bracket for block
identifiers.")#17
    msgs.append("One or more functions are missing a
'Return...' command.")#18
    msgs.append("Reserved words cannot be used for
variable names. Please change the following names in your
program.")#19
    msgs.append("Syntax for keyboard input command is
'Get string for...' ")#20
    msgs.append("Your file I/O command needs a '.txt' or
'.csv' suffix for the file name.")#21
    msgs.append("Your left-parentheses count does not
match your right-parentheses count.")#22
    msgs.append("The 'Return...' line must be immediately
followed by an 'End of function block.]' command.")#23
    return msgs


def display_msg(line, code, error_count):
    error_count += 1
    print(msgs[0],line,": ",msgs[code])
    return error_count


#Function to catch common errors and display error
messages.
#For each catch, the second argument in the call to
messages is the message index number.
def syntax_validation(KwicKode_file, msgs):
    is_valid = True
    error_count = 0
```

```
    block_starts = 0
    block_ends = 0
    left_brackets = 0
    right_brackets = 0
    left_parens = 0
    right_parens = 0
    function_count = 0
    return_count = 0
    if KwicKode_file[0][0:8] != "Comment:":
        error_count = display_msg(1, 1, error_count)
    for k in range(0, len(KwicKode_file)):
        line = str(k+1)
        xline = KwicKode_file[k][0:].strip()
        if xline == "" or xline == "\n":
            continue
        needs_period = True
        if xline.count("Comment:")==0 and
xline.count("Display")==0:
            left_brackets += xline.count("[")
            right_brackets += xline.count("]")
            left_parens += xline.count("(")
            right_parens += xline.count(")")
            if xline[0] == "[": block_starts += 1
            block_ends += xline.count("End of ")
            function_count += xline.count("[Function ")
            return_count += xline.count("Return ")
            if xline.count("End") != 0:
                needs_period = False
                if xline[-1:] != "]":
                    error_count = display_msg(line,
3, error_count)
                needs_period = False
            elif (xline.count("If") != 0 or
xline.count("Repeat")!=0 or \
                xline.count("Else")!=0 or
(xline.count("Function")!=0 and xline.count("Call")==0)):
                needs_period = False
                if (xline[-1:] != ":" or xline[0] !=
"["):
                    error_count = display_msg(line,
4, error_count)
```

```
                        needs_period = False
            if needs_period and xline[-1] != ".":
                error_count = display_msg(line, 2,
error_count)
            if xline[0:3] == "Get":
                if xline.count("Get string for ") == 0:
                    error_count = display_msg(line, 20,
error_count)
                if (k > 0) and (KwicKode_file[k-
1].count("Display ")== 0):
                    error_count = display_msg(line, 6,
error_count)
            if xline[1:4] == "If " and xline[-5:-1] !=
"then":
                error_count = display_msg(line, 7,
error_count)
            if xline[1:8] == "Repeat " and xline[7:14] != "
block ":
                error_count = display_msg(line, 8,
error_count)
            if xline[1:8] == "Repeat " and xline.count("
with ") != 1:
                error_count = display_msg(line, 8,
error_count)
            if (xline[0:10] == "Fill list "  and
xline.count(" and ") != 0):
                error_count = display_msg(line, 11,
error_count)
            if xline[0:10] == "[Function " and xline.count("
using ") != 1:
                error_count = display_msg(line, 12,
error_count)
            if xline[0:5] == "Call " and (xline.count(" with
")==0 or xline.count(" for ") == 0 ):
                    error_count = display_msg(line, 13,
error_count)
            if xline[0:8] == "Create " and (xline.count("
list ") == 0 and xline.count(" file ")) == 0:
                error_count = display_msg(line, 14,
error_count)
```

```
            if xline[0:12] == "Create file " and
(xline.count(".csv") == 0 and xline.count(".txt") == 0):
                erro_count = display_msg(line, 21,
error_count)
            if xline[0:5] == "Copy " and
(xline.count(".csv") == 0 and xline.count(".txt") == 0):
                error_count = display_msg(line, 21,
error_count)
            if xline[0:5] == "Copy " and (xline.count(" from
") == 0 and xline.count(" to ") == 0):
                error_count = display_msg(line, 15,
error_count)
            if xline[0:7] == ("Assign " or xline[0:5] ==
"copy ") and xline.count("list  ") > 0:
                error_count = display_msg(line, 9,
error_count)
            if xline[0:7] == "Return ":
                return_count += 1
                if (KwicKode_file[k+1].count("End of
function block.]")== 0):
                    error_count = display_msg(line,23,
error_count)
    line = "999"
    if block_starts > block_ends:
        error_count = display_msg(line, 5, error_count)
    if function_count > return_count:
        error_count = display_msg(line, 18, error_count)
    if left_brackets != right_brackets:
        error_count = display_msg(line, 16, error_count)
    if left_parens != right_parens:
        error_count = display_msg(line, 22, error_count)
    if error_count > 0:
        is_valid = False
        print("-------------------------------------------
----------------------------")
        print("The KwicKode compiler found
",error_count," error(s) in your program.")
        print("-------------------------------------------
----------------------------")

    return is_valid
```

```
#Function to catch reserved keywords being used as
variable names.
def variable_validation(KwicKode_file, var_names,
error_count):
    vars_ok = True
    bad_vars = []
    var_count = 0
    keywords = ["comment", "assign", "display", "get",
"if", "then",
                "else", "repeat", "block", "while",
"times", "end", "function",
                "with", "using", "create", "fill", "add",
                "remove", "from", "index", "value",
"data", "save", "file",
                "into", "to", "for", "return", "of",
"to",
                "print", "input", "def", "in", "range",
"elif", "import", "len", "str",
                "int", "float", "count", "append",
"remove", "shuffle", "pop", "index",
                "len", "random"]
    for k in range(0, len(var_names)):
        xline = KwicKode_file[k][0:-1].strip()
        for name in keywords:
            if var_names[k] == name:
                if bad_vars.count(var_names[k]) == 0:
                    bad_vars.append(var_names[k])
                    var_count += 1
    if var_count != 0:
        vars_ok = False
        line = ""
        error_count = display_msg(line, 19, error_count)
        for name in bad_vars:
            print("      "+name)
    return vars_ok


def parse_and_convert(KwicKode_file, var_names,
repeat_cntrs):
    '''This is the heart of the program. Each line in the
KwicKode file is read
```

```
       as xline, then, based on keywords in the line,
appropriate functions are called
       to create the Python code line(s) needed to affect
the desired command. Each line
       is stored in Python_file as zline.'''
       Python_file = []
       counter_count = 0
       indents = 0
       sp = "        "
       fatal_flaw = False
       # First check for any necessary modules to be
imported, but avoid
       # duplicate occurences.
       imps = ["V","R","I","C","S","M"]
       for k in range(0, len(KwicKode_file)):
              if KwicKode_file[k].count(".csv") != 0 and "V"
in imps:
                     Python_file.append("import csv")
                     imps.remove("V")
              if KwicKode_file[k].count("random(") != 0 and
"R" in imps:
                     Python_file.append("from random import
random")
                     imps.remove("R")
              if KwicKode_file[k].count("randint(") != 0 and
"I" in imps:
                     Python_file.append("from random import
randint")
                     imps.remove("I")
              if KwicKode_file[k].count("choice(") != 0 and
"C" in imps:
                     Python_file.append("from random import
choice")
                     imps.remove("C")
              if KwicKode_file[k].count("shuffle(") != 0 and
"S" in imps:
                     Python_file.append("from random import
shuffle")
                     imps.remove("S")
              if KwicKode_file[k].count("math.") != 0 and "M"
in imps:
```

```
            Python_file.append("import math")
            imps.remove("M")
      # Now loop through KwicKode file line by line for
translation to Python.
      # Indentation is removed (strip function) and periods
are deleted.
      for k in range(0, len(KwicKode_file)):
            xline = KwicKode_file[k][0:-1].strip()
            zline = ""
            #Duplicate blank lines for the Python code.
            if xline == "" or xline == "\n":
                  Python_file.append("")
                  continue
            x = xline[-1:]
            #Variable indents accounts for program blocks,
but watch for index brackets.
            if xline[0] == "[":
                  indents += 1 #requires use of indents-1 for
first line of block.
            elif xline[-7:] == "block.]":
                  indents -= 1 #since this line deleted for
Python, no adjustment needed except for
                              #repeats, where user-defined
loop counter must be incremented.
            if xline[0:14] == "End of repeat ":
                  cntr = repeat_cntrs.pop()
                  zline = sp*(indents+1)+ cntr + " += 1"
                  Python_file.append(zline)
            #The 16 KwicKode commands are each dealt with in
order, most with a function call.
            if xline[0:8] == "Comment:":
Python_file.append(sp*indents + "# " + xline[9:])
            elif xline[0:7] == "Display":
display_parser(xline, Python_file, sp, indents)
            elif xline[0:15] == "Get string for ":
input_parser(xline, var_names, Python_file, sp, indents)
            elif xline[0:6] == "Assign":
assign_parser(xline, var_names, Python_file, sp, indents)
            elif xline[0:8] == "[Repeat ":
repeat_parser(xline, var_names, Python_file, sp, indents,
repeat_cntrs)
```

```
        elif xline[1:3] == "If": Python_file.append(
sp*(indents-1) + "if (" + xline[4:-5] + "):")
        elif xline[1:5] == "Else":  Python_file.append(
sp*(indents-1) + "else:")
        elif xline[0:11] == "Create list":
create_list_parser(xline, var_names, Python_file, sp,
indents)
        elif xline[0:3] == "Add": append_parser(xline,
var_names, Python_file, sp, indents)
        elif xline[0:6] == "Remove":
remove_parser(xline, Python_file, sp, indents)
        elif xline[1:9] == "Function":
function_parser(xline, var_names, Python_file, sp,
indents)
        elif xline[0:4] == "Call":
function_call_parser(xline, var_names, Python_file, sp,
indents)
        elif xline[0: 6] == "Return":
Python_file.append(sp*indents + "return " + xline[6:-1])
        elif xline[0:11] == "Create file":
create_file_parser(xline, Python_file, sp, indents)
        elif xline[0:9] == "Copy data":
fileops_parser(xline, Python_file, sp, indents)
    if fatal_flaw:
        Python_file = [fatal_flaw]
    return(Python_file)

def display_parser(xline, Python_file, sp, ind):
    ''' Display command, Display .... ( as list.)'''
    aslst = xline[-9:]
    if aslst == " as list.":
        objct = xline[8:-8]
        yline = sp*ind + "works = True"
        Python_file.append(yline)
        yline = sp*ind + "try:"
        Python_file.append(yline)
        yline = sp*(ind+1) + "lngth = len("+objct+")"
        Python_file.append(yline)
        yline = sp*ind + "except TypeError:"
        Python_file.append(yline)
        yline = sp*(ind+1)+"works = False"
```

```python
        Python_file.append(yline)
        yline = sp*(ind+1)+"print(" + objct+")"
        Python_file.append(yline)
        yline = sp*ind+"if works == True:"
        Python_file.append(yline)
        yline = sp*(ind+1) + "for i in range(0,
len("+objct + ")):"
        Python_file.append(yline)
        yline = sp*(ind+2)+"print("+objct+"[i])"
    else:
        yline = sp*(ind)+"print(" + xline[8:-1]+")"
    Python_file.append(yline)
    return


def input_parser(xline, var_names, Python_file, sp,ind):
    ''' Parser for Get string for... command to Python
input, with prompt.'''
    prompt = Python_file.pop()
    prompt = prompt[ind*5+6:-1]
    zline = sp*ind + xline[15:-1] + " = input(" + prompt
+ ")"
    Python_file.append(zline)
    var_names.append(xline[15:-1])
    return


def assign_parser(xline, var_names, Python_file, sp, ind):
    ''' Assignment command, Assign...to .... or Assign
...to list...'''
    a = 0
    target = ""
    for k in range(len(xline)-1,0,-1):
        if xline[k:k+4] == " to ":
            a = k
            if xline[k:k+9] == " to list ":
                target = xline[k+9:-1]
            else:
                target = xline[k+4:-1]
        if a != 0: break
    obj = xline[7:a]
    if xline[a:a+9] == " to list ":
        zline = sp*ind + target + " = [" + obj + "]"
```

```
    else:
        zline = sp*ind + target + " = " + obj
    Python_file.append(zline)
    var_names.append(target)
    return


def repeat_parser(xline, var_names, Python_file, sp, ind,
repeat_cntrs):
    '''Parser for [Repeat block while ...with ...: is
covered here.'''
    a = xline.find(" with ")
    ind -=1
    cntr = xline[a+6:-1]
    repeat_cntrs.append(cntr)
    yline = sp*(ind) + cntr + " = 0"
    Python_file.append(yline)
    yline = sp*ind + "while " + xline[20:a] + ":"
    Python_file.append(yline)
    var_names.append(cntr)
    return


def create_list_parser(xline, var_names, Python_file, sp,
ind):
    ''' Convert KwicKode Creat list var_name. into
Python.'''
    a = xline.find(" list ")
    list_name = xline[a+6:-1]
    zline = sp*ind + list_name + " = []"
    Python_file.append(zline)
    var_names.append(list_name)
    return


def append_parser(xline, var_names, Python_file, sp, ind):
    ''' Convert KwicKode Add xxx to list var_name. into
Python.'''
    a = 0
    for k in range(len(xline)-1,0,-1):
        if xline[k:k+4] == " to ":
            a = k
            target = xline[k+9:-1]
        if a != 0: break
```

```python
    obj = xline[4:a]
    zline = sp*ind + target + ".extend([" + obj + "])"
    Python_file.append(zline)
    var_names.append(target)
    return

def remove_parser(xline,Python_file, sp, ind ):
    '''Convert KwicKode Remove xxx from list var_name.
into Python.'''
    a = 0
    for k in range(len(xline)-1,0,-1):
        if xline[k:k+6] == " from ":
            a = k
            target = xline[k+11:-1]
        if a != 0: break
    obj = xline[7:a]
    zline = sp*ind + "try:"
    Python_file.append(zline)
    zline = sp*(ind+1) + target + ".remove(" + obj + ")"
    Python_file.append(zline)
    zline = sp*ind + "except ValueError:"
    Python_file.append(zline)
    zline = sp*(ind+1) + "print("+obj+", 'was not
found.')"
    Python_file.append(zline)
    return

def function_parser(xline, var_names, Python_file, sp, ind
):
    '''Convert KwicKode [Function name using (...): into
Python.'''
    a = xline.find(" using ")
    function_name = xline[10:a]
    parameters = xline[a+8:-2]
    zline = sp*(ind-1)+"def " + function_name + "(" +
parameters + "):"
    Python_file.append(zline)
    var_names.append(function_name)
    return
```

```
def function_call_parser(xline, var_names, Python_file,
sp, ind):
    '''Convert KwicKode Call function xxx with ... for
yyy. into Python.'''
    a = xline.find(" with ")
    b = xline.find(" for ")
    function_name = xline[14:a]
    arguments = xline[a+6:b]
    target = xline[b+5:-1]
    zline = sp*ind + target + " = " + function_name +
arguments
    Python_file.append(zline)
    var_names.append(target)
    return

def create_file_parser(xline, Python_file, sp, ind):
    '''Creates an empty .csv or .txt file, or empties an
existing one from
        command: Create file xxx.'''
    file_name = xline[12:-1]
    zline = sp*ind + "outfile = open('" + file_name
+"','w')"
    Python_file.append(zline)
    zline = sp*ind + "outfile.close()"
    Python_file.append(zline)
    return

def fileops_parser(xline, Python_file, sp, ind):
    '''Handles file I/O from Copy data from xxx to yyy.
Determines which is
        the file by looking for .csv or .txt suffix.'''
    a = xline.find(" from ")
    b = xline.find(" to ")
    suffix1 = xline[-5:-1]
    suffix2 = xline[b-4:b]
    if suffix1 == ".txt" or suffix1 == ".csv":
        savedata_parser(xline, Python_file, sp, ind)
    elif suffix2 == ".txt" or suffix2 == ".csv":
        getdata_parser(xline, Python_file, sp, ind)
    return
```

```python
def savedata_parser(xline, Python_file, sp, ind):
    '''Saves list data in a .txt or .csv file. Creates
the file if doesnt exist.
    Subsequent data appended (as separate list) onto the
previous data.
    KwicKode command: Copy data from xxx to yyy. where
yyy is the data file. '''
    a = xline.find(" from ")
    b = xline.find(" to ")
    file_name = xline[b+4:-1]
    list_name = xline[a+6:b]
    if file_name[-4:] == ".txt":
        zline = sp*ind + "with open('"+file_name+"',
mode='a', newline='\\n') as outfile:"
        Python_file.append(zline)
        zline = sp*(ind+1) + "for item in
"+list_name+":"
        Python_file.append(zline)
        zline = sp*(ind+2)+"outfile.write(item + '\\n')"
        Python_file.append(zline)
    else:
        zline = sp*ind + "with open('"+file_name+"',
mode='a', newline='') as outfile:"
        Python_file.append(zline)
        zline = sp*(ind+1)+"record =
csv.writer(outfile)"
        Python_file.append(zline)
        if xline[5:13] == "database":
            zline =
sp*(ind+1)+"record.writerows("+list_name+")"
            Python_file.append(zline)
        else:
            zline = sp*(ind+1)+
"record.writerow("+list_name+")"
            Python_file.append(zline)
    zline = sp*(ind+1) + "outfile.close()"
    Python_file.append(zline)
    return

def getdata_parser(xline, Python_file, sp, ind):
```

```
    '''Retrieve data from a .csv  or .txt file, or
display an error message if the file
    does not exist.
    KwicKode command: Copy data from xxx to yyy. where
xxx is the data file.'''
    a = xline.find(" from ")
    b = xline.find(" to ")
    file_name = xline[a+6:b]
    list_name = xline[b+4:-1]
    zline = sp*ind + "file_found = True"
    Python_file.append(zline)
    zline = sp*ind + list_name + " = []"
    Python_file.append(zline)
    zline = sp*ind + "try:"
    Python_file.append(zline)
    zline = sp*(ind+1) + "with open('" + file_name +
"','r', newline='') as infile:"
    Python_file.append(zline)
    zline = sp*(ind+2) + "infile.close()"
    Python_file.append(zline)
    zline = sp*ind + "except FileNotFoundError:"
    Python_file.append(zline)
    zline = sp*(ind+1) + "print('There is no such
file.')"
    Python_file.append(zline)
    zline = sp*(ind+1)+ "file_found = False"
    Python_file.append(zline)
    zline = sp*ind + "if file_found == True:"
    Python_file.append(zline)
    zline = sp*(ind+1) + "with open('" + file_name +
"','r', newline='') as infile:"
    Python_file.append(zline)
    if file_name[-4:] == ".csv":
        zline = sp*(ind+2) + "records =
csv.reader(infile)"
        Python_file.append(zline)
        if xline[5:13] == "database":
            zline = sp*(ind+2) + list_name + " = [row
for row in records]"
            Python_file.append(zline)
        else:
```

```
                zline = sp*(ind+2) + "for record in
records:"
                Python_file.append(zline)
                zline = sp*(ind+3) + list_name +
".extend(record)"
                Python_file.append(zline)
        else:
            zline = sp*(ind+2) + "records =
infile.readlines()"
            Python_file.append(zline)
            zline = sp*(ind+2) + "for record in records:"
            Python_file.append(zline)
            zline = sp*(ind+3) + list_name +
".append(record[0:-1])"
            Python_file.append(zline)
        zline = sp*(ind+2)+"infile.close()"
        Python_file.append(zline)
        return


def retrieve_data(filename1, text_input):
    '''Open text file and store entire program in
text_input.'''
    file_exists = True
    try:
        infile = open(filename1, "r+")
    except FileNotFoundError:
        print("There is no file with that name.")
        file_exists = False
    if file_exists:
        text_input = infile.readlines()
        infile.close()
    return text_input


def save_data(text_output, filename2):
    '''Append one record (variable or list) to the
database text file.'''
    outfile = open(filename2, "w")
    for k in range(0,len(text_output)):
        outfile.write(text_output[k]+"\n")
    outfile.close()
    return
```

```
#---------------------------------------------------
#Main Program
KwicKode_file = []
Python_file = []
var_names = []
errs = []
repeat_cntrs = []
msgs = []
msgs = load_msgs(msgs)

program_filename = get_KwicKode_filename()
python_program = program_filename[0:-4]+".py"

KwicKode_file =
retrieve_data(program_filename,KwicKode_file)

is_valid = True
vars_ok = True
is_valid = syntax_validation(KwicKode_file, msgs)
if (is_valid == True ):
    Python_file = parse_and_convert(KwicKode_file,
var_names, repeat_cntrs)
    vars_ok = True
    vars_ok = variable_validation(KwicKode_file,
var_names, 0)
if vars_ok == True and is_valid == True:
    if len(Python_file) > 1:
        try:
            save_data(Python_file, python_program)
            print("Your Python program named
",(program_filename[0:-4]+".py")," is ready to run.")
        except TypeError:
            print("Your KwicKode program has a
problem.")
else: print("Please correct the problem(s) and try
again.")
```

About the Author

Dan Bishop received his Ph.D. degree in organic chemistry from the University of Kansas and spent his career teaching various chemistry courses and computer science classes. After he retired from Colorado State University in Fort Collins, he was employed by a defense contractor as a programming engineer on a satellite services contract for the U.S. Air Force while waiting for his wife Ann to join him in retirement.

He and his wife now live with their black cat Mario in a small mountain town in central Colorado where he divides his time between writing, gardening, and painting landscapes and abstracts, in addition to being an active volunteer in local organizations.

Promoting STEM programs and encouraging students to pursue careers in chemistry and computer science remains a focus in his life. KwicKode is a project he tackled to address the frustration many students have with beginning computer science courses. He believes that KwicKode, with its reduced instruction set and simplified syntax, will help more students to achieve success in their initial foray into programming. He sees KwicKode as a springboard into further studies in computer science and careers in computing and other science and engineering fields.

authordbishop@gmail.com

www.authordbishop.com